Praise for *A Ye...*

"This book is both hardhead... ers and aspiring writers that they aren't the only ones caught up in this glorious delusion — that we can write, and that it will not only heal us but will make the world better."

— Carolyn See, author of *Making a Literary Life*

"This book is intelligent, generous, compassionate, and true. It's like getting a whole lifetime of writing wisdom packed into one year. I loved it."

— Jennie Nash, author of *The Threadbare Heart* and *The Victoria's Secret Catalog Never Stops Coming: And Other Lessons I Learned from Breast Cancer*

"I loved this book. Every entry is a new adventure, followed by a quotation that illuminates and stimulates the mind. Hooray for Barbara Abercrombie!"

— Abigail Thomas, author of *A Three Dog Life*

"Exuberant writing-whisperer Barbara Abercrombie fills her infectiously joyous book with insider writing advice, quotes, confidences, and support that will inspire, cajole, and jump-start every writing muscle in your heart and soul. Funny and full of comfort (and the company of writing rock stars), this book is as essential to a writer as a verb."

— Caroline Leavitt, *New York Times* bestselling author of *Pictures of You*

"If you are a writer — and go on, be brave, say, 'I am a writer' — then this is the book you will turn to every morning, noon, or night when you sit down to write. These are the words that will inspire you, that will chivvy you along, and that will remind you that, come what may, you have no choice — you must write. Barbara Abercrombie is an amazing teacher, and with this book you've just joined her class — which meets every single day. Congratulations. Now read on — and write."

— Jacqueline Winspear, author of the Maisie Dobbs mystery series

"When you open Barbara Abercrombie's brilliant *A Year of Writing Dangerously*, you are in a house full of writers, each of whom wants to march you over to a corner to tell you something important about the writing life. The charm of this book lies in Abercrombie's impeccable taste in the writers she chooses and the way she deftly wraps her own thoughts around each entry so that it becomes a memoir of one writer presiding over a feast of writers. Prepare yourself for a wonderful party! Then start writing."

— Phyllis Theroux, author of *The Journal Keeper: A Memoir*

"Barbara Abercrombie's new book manages to be both candid and inspiring. Full of the kind of wit and wisdom her students have come to expect and her lucky readers will surely treasure."

— Dennis Palumbo, psychotherapist and author of the Daniel Rinaldi mystery series

"I love the title of this collection of writerly wisdom, because writing is dangerous, and we need courage to face that danger day by day. *A Year of Writing Dangerously* gives us courage and inspiration in 365 little gems. Reading this book is like having an old friend in the room or a box of divine chocolates, each wrapped in gold foil, each with a surprising nugget at its center. There is something necessary in these pages for everyone, from the beginning writer to the widely published author. I will keep this book close at hand for those many moments when I will need it."

— Naomi Benaron, author of *Running the Rift*, winner of the Bellwether Prize for Fiction

"This is a lovely book — beautifully written, beautifully thought. But that wouldn't be enough, would it, to make it necessary? So let me add: this is a tremendously useful book for anyone who wants to write — and for any time in that person's life, whether just beginning or already well published. By the time I got to page 15, I already had six writing friends on my list to give it to, and the book has more than 365 pages! It is a daybook, something to keep on one's desk and beside the bed. This book is a friend, and will be one long after the year is up. It speaks lasting truths in a wise voice."

— Janet Sternburg, author of *Phantom Limb*

A Year of
Writing Dangerously

Also by the Author

A Year of Writing Dangerously

365 Days
of Inspiration
& Encouragement

BARBARA ABERCROMBIE

New World Library
Novato, California

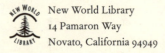 New World Library
14 Pamaron Way
Novato, California 94949

Text design by Tona Pearce-Myers

Library of Congress Cataloging-in-Publication Data
Abercrombie, Barbara.
 A year of writing dangerously : 365 days of inspiration & encouragement / Barbara Abercrombie.
    p.   cm.
Includes bibliographical references.
ISBN 978-1-60868-051-1 (pbk. : alk. paper)
1. Authorship. I. Title.
PN145.A26 2012
808.02—dc23   2012009880

First printing, June 2012
ISBN 978-1-60868-051-1
Printed in Canada on 100% postconsumer-waste recycled paper

 New World Library is proud to be a Gold Certified Environmentally Responsible Publisher. Publisher certification awarded by Green Press Initiative. www.greenpressinitiative.org

10 9 8 7 6 5 4 3 2 1

For Emma, Axel, and Grace

Contents

I write to discover. I write to uncover. I write to meet my ghosts....
I write because it is dangerous, a bloody risk, like love, to form the
words.

— TERRY TEMPEST WILLIAMS

The room, you see, is a dangerous place. Not in itself, but because
you're dangerous. The psyche is dangerous. Every single word is
full of secrets, full of associations, every word leads to another and
another and another, down and down, through passages of dark
and light.

— MICHAEL VENTURA

Introduction

Why a year?

Because if you want to write a novel or a memoir or an autobiography you'll need at least a year of focused work to get from the idea in your head to the reality of a first draft. Or if you want to write short pieces, a year could get you from dreaming about being a writer to actually completing and marketing one or more personal essays or short stories. This is a book about writing your way through 365 days.

Why dangerously?

Because there's always a sense of risk when you write — fear that maybe someone will deny your version of things, or that they'll get mad and disown you, or that maybe you'll make a fool of yourself and expose too much or too little. Writing your own truth, even under the veils and masks of fiction, will always feel dangerous. It will also feel liberating.

Why write?

Because you have to. You have to write down this story

that's banging around in your head and in your heart or it'll be lost. No one else will tell it. And it'll just keep banging or humming away in there, driving you nuts. These are your thoughts and your feelings, your imagination and your memories. This is how you put the vast chaos of your life into order, how you get to the other side. Writing is also how you nail down and get to keep the good moments. How you live more deeply and become more conscious.

My hope is that this book will provide you with day-by-day inspiration to help you get your story told – from writing down the first sentence, to finding the time to write, on through the months of many drafts and possible discouragement, right up until the end of the year, when your story could be ready to send out into the world. This isn't a how-to book because no book can really teach you how to write. The only way you learn to write is by reading and studying the kind of thing you would like to write — and by writing.

Or maybe you've been writing for years and are simply in a temporary funk and need to get unstuck. In any case, this is a *why* book. No matter where we are in our writing, we need to be reminded, sometimes day by day, why we're writing, why we ever wanted to do this in the first place, why it's important and why we feel so antsy and crazy when we're not writing. The why of writing is answered by other writers, a whole chorus of writers whose words can inspire us to get into action and to keep going. Determination is an inside job, but inspiration comes from the outside.

Or maybe you're not antsy and crazy and just happen to be in a rare group of calm, secure, and dignified individuals who simply want to write their story. That's fine, and I hope you'll find all the encouragement you need in this book. However, a little desperation and unsettledness certainly never hurt a writer; we all go through strange and painful periods in our lives and one of the reasons we read is to find out how other people, real or fictional, navigate the hard times.

Sometimes writing prompts can help you get started when you're stuck; they can knock down walls and lead you into surprising and deeper territory. At the end of the book there are fifty-two writing prompts, one for each week of the year, that can be used for writing either fiction or memoir and essays.

I like to think of this book as a party. Come on in and meet writers who will offer interesting ideas, hold your hand, be right there at your elbow when you have the urge to throw your laptop out the window, writers who have some smart, funny, and inspirational takes on what it means to find the courage to write.

One year. Why not?

365 Days
of Dangerous
Writing

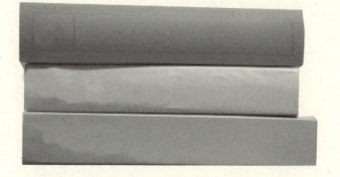

1. Switchbacks up the Mountain

When I'm stuck and scared to death of writing the first line, I drive up to a cabin I have two hours north of Los Angeles. The highway up the mountain, while a perfectly good road and well maintained, and in fact traveled by hundreds of people daily, is nevertheless dangerous; it goes from sea level to 5,800 feet with some scary switchbacks. A lot of awful accidents have occurred on this road, but it's the only way up.

My cabin, which sounds romantic in theory but isn't, has had its own dangerous moments: rocks thrown through windows by vandals; pipes freezing and then bursting, which caused a ceiling to fall in; a forest fire that stopped down the road just in time; a burglar who stole some totally useless speakers and an old computer during an evacuation for the above-mentioned fire; and in winter when it snows, the driveway fills up with huge drifts, and getting to the front door feels like you're hiking over frozen tundra somewhere north of Canada.

Whenever I arrive up there, I'm grateful that I made it, and relieved if my cabin is standing unharmed and there aren't five-foot snowdrifts blocking my driveway. I bumble around for a while, light-headed from altitude, with the silence bouncing off the walls and filling me with dread. Eventually I realize there's nothing else to do up here but to open my laptop and start writing. Writing has always felt just like that road up, scary, full of dangerous switchbacks. Writing holds the possibility that I won't have anything to say, not another word. That perhaps my imagination has dried up and my brain is empty.

We all have our own road up the mountain, or down into the valley, or in a small rickety boat over deep and dark water. Pick your metaphor. There's no way to glide gracefully into writing, no way to hide who we really are. There's always that loud space of emptiness and silence when you start to write, whether you're in a cabin or your bedroom or an office. There's no way to guarantee a safe, easy journey into words on the page. It's just you and your memory and experience and imagination. Naked.

So up in my cabin, I put on some CDs, something loud and cheerful and raucous. If it's cold, I light a fire in the fireplace; if it's warm, I sit out on the deck and breathe in the pine trees. Then I read something that will inspire me, remind me why I'm up here without all the props of modern life and why I want to write in the first place. And pretty soon I feel calm enough to open my laptop. And I start writing.

I suffer as always from the fear of putting down the first line. It is amazing the terrors, the magics, the prayers, the straitening shyness that assail one.

— John Steinbeck

2. Sacred Space

The date you begin writing, or start a new book, should be memorable, like a wedding date or a birthday.

Sure you can suddenly fly to your computer exclaiming today you start your book, your essay! But preparing for the day, suddenly yearning for the day, making it important, builds up energy for writing. Clearing your space, desk, table, or wherever you're going to write, setting up objects or photographs you love, and making it inviting might be a good way to begin. You're courting the muse, after all.

Take time to get ready. Find books by writers you love, writers who inspire you.

Figure out what time you'll write. On your calendar put a slash through that time slot so you won't inadvertently plan something else.

In the end, wherever and whenever you work, make your writing time and your work space sacred.

I tell my students one of the most important things they need to know is when they are at their best, creatively. They need to ask themselves, What does the ideal room look like? Is there music? Is there silence? Is there chaos outside or is there serenity outside? What do I need in order to release my imagination?

— Toni Morrison

3. The Holy Calling

You may find that your friends and family are somewhat less than respectful of your sitting there in your sacred space. They might even refer to what you're up to as "typing" or "your new hobby." Writing is not a hobby. Collecting stamps or coins is a hobby. Writing is a calling.

I believe that — if you are serious about a life of writing, or indeed about any creative form of expression — you should take on this work like a holy calling. I became a writer the way other people become monks or nuns....I was writing's most devotional handmaiden. I built my entire life around writing.

— ELIZABETH GILBERT

4. Choosing Story over Relatives

Isabel Allende begins all her books on January 8. She says that she writes the first sentence and then the story begins to unfold. One particular January 8 at the crack of dawn, her agent, Carmen Balcells, called her from Spain and told her to write a memoir.

Allende replied that her family didn't like to see itself exposed.

"Don't worry about anything," said Balcells. "Send me a two- or three-hundred-page letter and I'll take care of the rest. If it comes down to choosing between telling a story and offending relatives, any professional writer chooses the former."

Allende went on to write the memoir, but she struggled with having protagonists that were her "own living family, filled with opinions and conflicts." The plot was "not an exercise of imagination but an attempt to present the truth."

As you write, you might want to keep this thought in mind: *No one will read what you're writing until you allow them to.* So you are free to write the truth, or whatever you believe to be the truth. You can write dreadful and shocking things from your imagination, you can write badly and sloppily, you can whine and mewl if you want. Because *you can always rewrite, change things, or simply tear it up.*

Writing is rewriting. But first you need to have something on the page to rewrite.

And so I began to write about things I thought I would never tell another soul as long as I lived.

— MAY-LEE CHAI

5. Getting Caught

I asked a group of students once if writing felt dangerous to them. They all nodded vigorously, so I asked them to write why.

One student wrote, "Writing is dangerous because you might get caught."

Caught, found out, exposed. The stuff of nightmares.

Is this why writing feels so scary sometimes? We're caught like a fish on the hook of our own words, our secrets exposed, our inner life and imagination up for inspection.

Anxiety is not only an inevitable part of the writing process but a necessary part. If you're not scared, you're not writing.

— RALPH KEYES

6. Daring to Tell

Here's another response, from a student, to my question about why writing feels dangerous: "Sometimes it feels dangerous to know what I really feel. Because if I acknowledge my feelings outside the safe boundaries of my own heart and mind, if I open up the latch to my subconscious and let those precious secrets leak out, God knows what will happen. I might have to hold myself accountable to these thoughts and feelings. I might have to act upon them. I might have to change. I might have to stop lying to myself and others about what I need and want. I might have to ask for what I need and want. I might have to be a disappointment; I might have to be disappointed; I will disappoint."

This quote and the previous one were not written by people who had been hiding in caves for the past decade. They are both very successful professional people and in positions of power and respect, one a doctor and one a religious leader.

We are all scared of disappointing, of venturing past the safe boundaries of our minds and hearts — those of us still hiding in our caves and those of us whose job it is to help others. We all go around wearing masks.

You know, we do live in ludicrous ignorance of each other. I mean, we usually don't know the things we'd like to know even about our supposedly closest friends. I mean, suppose you're going through some kind of hell in your own life, well, you would love to know if your friends have experienced similar things. But we really don't dare to ask each other.

— WALLACE SHAWN and ANDRÉ GREGORY,
My Dinner with André

7. Jumping Off

There's no appropriate place, no safe place to jump off into your writing. In his writing classes, Roger Rosenblatt bursts into singing "Happy Birthday" out of nowhere, and his students stare at him as if he's gone around the bend. He sings it again, and then tells them to start writing as they hear in their heads this "irritating, celebratory song you've heard all your lives." Then he sings it yet again for them, and they lean forward and begin to write.

But the jumping-off place isn't always so obvious. You can't always find the way in. Sometimes you need a side door.

— ABIGAIL THOMAS

8. The Voice That Chirps and Chips

We're so good with the negative voices: *You idiot, what kind of an idea is that? Who do you think you are to be writing a book? Why are you sitting there in your bedroom slippers writing about your boring life? Who cares?* When that voice starts chirping in your head and chipping away at your confidence, here's what you do: Listen to another voice, the sweet, calm voice that's saying, *Just do the work. Tell your story; it's important. Have faith.* If you're sitting at Starbucks or at the library, it's probably best not to say this out loud, but if you're home alone — say it loud. And often.

Know that it is good to work. Work with love and think of liking it when you do it. It is easy and interesting. It is a privilege. There is nothing hard about it but your anxious vanity and fear of failure.
— BRENDA UELAND

9. Getting Permission

When William Zinsser visited schools to discuss writing, he'd ask students, "What are your problems? What are your concerns?" and suggest that this would be the subject of their writing. But from grade school to college, most students would tell him that they didn't have permission to write about themselves; the teachers gave them the subjects to write about.

Established writers would tell him they had to write what editors wanted.

If this has a familiar ring to you, or if you feel you need permission to write about yourself or whatever you need to write about, I give you permission.

Now you have it. Use it.

If you write for yourself, you'll reach all the people you want to write for.

— WILLIAM ZINSSER

10. Working Out

I give a lot of five-minute exercises when I teach, because I think writing for just five minutes forces you to get out of your own way and lets you off the hook for writing something brilliant. Five minutes — no pausing, no stopping! Who could come up with something even readable in such a short time? But it's amazing what can happen. People come up with memories or feelings or thoughts they didn't even know they had. And if they don't come up with anything they can use, so what? I do this exercise when I'm stuck with my own writing. I'll write a character's name or one word or idea at the top of the page and just start writing. I don't think — I write. Sometimes you need to let yourself go off into uncharted territory.

I have a student who's a successful mystery novelist and who knows everything she really needs to know about writing and discipline, but she shows up periodically in class to do writing exercises, to work out; she calls the class her writing gym.

Everybody else works out — actors, musicians, dancers — why not writers?

So let's pick up the pen, and kick some ass. Write down who you were, who you are, and what you remember.

— Natalie Goldberg

11. Racing Hearts and Churning Stomachs

M. came to class eight years ago, flew into class, really, scared to death. When it was her turn to read in the workshop session, she panicked and fluttered and almost flew back out of the room. "I don't know what I'm writing!" she said. "I don't know if it's fiction or memoir. It's awful! I can't read it!"

"Just read," I said. And she did. Well, it wasn't awful. It was funny and weird, and we wanted to hear more. "Just keep writing," I said. She did. She brought back true stories of her life that made us laugh and cry. And she eventually got her memoir published by a big publisher in New York. Then she started another book, and one morning flew back into class, still scared, saying, "Well, I knew I had to bring something to read, so I brought this, this — mess. But I'm too embarrassed to read it."

"Just read," I said. And she did and it was wonderful. "Just keep writing," I said.

She agonized over what her family would say, think, do. What they did was get really, really mad. She changed her name and forged on.

When her second memoir came out, I went to a big party in Hollywood that her publisher threw for her. There was an open bar and little hot crab things and platters of cheeses and breads and sausages, and even *pommes frites*. (You have to understand how amazing this is because most of us writers, should we be lucky enough to get a book published and a bookstore to give us time and space, throw our own parties with Trader Joe's wine and baskets of pretzels.)

I tell you about M. because she was so scared, so insecure

in the beginning (and in fact still is with every new piece of writing), but she didn't let that fear and insecurity stop her.

So know that you don't have to "like" your own writing. You don't have to be calm and self-assured. In fact, it's better if you're not. It keeps you honest.

Finding the courage to write does not involve erasing or "conquering" one's fears. Working writers aren't those who have eliminated their anxiety. They are the ones who keep scribbling while their heart races and their stomach churns.

— Ralph Keyes

12. Patience

No one has to be patient anymore. We can publish books right from our computers. We can get messages anywhere, anytime. We can have whole libraries of books instantly zapped to whatever our latest gadget is, or a complete film festival delivered at the click of a button. We can plug ourselves directly into our music without bothering with CDs. We never, ever have to be bored, subjected to silence, or deal with our inner life.

But no matter how fast the world zips along, no matter how much fun there is to be had, the fact remains that writing takes time. To write takes dreaming and remembering and thinking and imagining — and very often what feels like wasting time. It takes silence and solitude. It takes being okay with making a huge mess and not knowing what you're doing. Then it takes rewriting and struggling to find your story and the truth of the story, and then the meaning of the story. It takes being comfortable with your own doubts and fears and questions. And there's just no fast and easy way around it.

The essential question is, "Have you found a space, that empty space, which should surround you when you write?" Into that space, which is like a form of listening, of attention, will come the words your characters will speak, ideas — inspiration.

— DORIS LESSING

13. The Matanuska Valley and Other Diversions

Research for your writing can be great fun; it can also be a cozy little trap. I once spent a blissful month researching Alaska for a project I can no longer remember and never actually wrote. I became particularly fascinated with the Matanuska Valley, where vegetables grow ten times their usual size because of the abundance and slant of the sunlight. For over a month I happily made notes, thrilled that I didn't have to actually write. I just copied down facts about giant vegetables.

Libraries and the Internet can be like crack houses for the research addicted. What's hard, messy, and frustrating is writing words straight out of your own head.

I'm a real believer in research, but I have a funny way of doing it. I think you should write first and then *do the research.*

— MONA SIMPSON

14. Waiting for Pizza

You can find ideas in the strangest places. For instance, the Shack in Twin Bridges, Montana. They serve the best pizza in the world, and they keep piles of old magazines on the tables to read while you wait for your pizza. One cold winter afternoon as I waited, I discovered "50 Things to Do to Improve Your Life" in an ancient copy of *U.S. News & World Report*. One of the things to do was "make yourself an author." As an example, they used five sisters who put together their recipes and cooking stories, self-published them, and sold five hundred copies. Another thing to do was to keep a simple diary: "Distill your day's experience into a single sentence each day. Call it a 'coat hanger' journal. It provides a framework on which to hang the larger raiments of memory."

Carry a notebook with you. Look for ideas. You never know where you'll find them.

For at least thirty years, and at almost all times, I have carried a notebook with me, in my back pocket.

— MARY OLIVER

15. People in a Jam

In his introduction to *Good Poems for Hard Times*, Garrison Keillor writes: "The meaning of poetry is to give courage. A poem is not a puzzle that you the dutiful reader are obliged to solve. It is meant to poke you, get you to buck up, pay attention, rise and shine, look alive, get a grip.... The intensity of poetry, its imaginative fervor, its cadences, is not meant for the triumphant executive, but for people in a jam — you and me."

And aren't we all in a jam more or less?

I start every class I teach by reading a poem; it's like a secular prayer. It gets us right down to what's important — feelings, ideas, language.

When words feel old, dried up, and empty, when *you* feel old, dried up, and empty, read a poet you love. Feel how poems can, yes, poke you, buck you up, give you courage, and how you can fall in love with language, metaphor, and images. How a poem can say something that it could take a whole novel to get across. But skip the poets you don't understand and who make your head hurt. Life is short.

When I first wanted to be a writer, I learned to write prose by reading poetry.

— NICHOLSON BAKER

16. Exploding Typewriters, Smoking Computers

There's a museum in a vineyard in Napa, California, with an exhibit of a typewriter on fire. The fire is real and continuous, sort of pyromaniac performance art. I was with a daughter when I saw it, and she burst into laughter. She said probably only a writer's kid would find it that funny.

Annie Dillard wrote about having a typewriter that erupted, exploding with sparks and ash, and then flames. Did this really happen or was it a metaphor? How can a typewriter burn and then, as she claims, cause no more trouble?

I had a computer once that threatened to explode. Smoke poured out of it. It grew hot. Or did I imagine that? I was unable to write at the time, I felt I had no voice, nothing to say, so perhaps I was hallucinating or giving myself an excuse not to write. Or maybe all this has something to do with the danger of writing.

Discover your voice. Determine how it is different from all other voices. Make it hot for yourself. Get into trouble. Go to where the jeopardy is.

— Gordon Lish

17. Love Thy Reader

Whatever word you want to wrap around this idea — *love, respect, trust* — the point is that you need to believe your reader deserves the very best you have to offer and is every bit as smart as you are. The reader gives you his or her time, which is just as precious as yours, and will pay good money to read your story. Readers deserve to be treated like your closest friends, people you're compelled to tell the truth to.

The first thing a writer must do is love the reader and wish the reader well....Only in such well wishing and trust, only when the writer feels he is writing a letter to a good friend, only then will the magic happen.

— ELLEN GILCHRIST

18. Your Validation Posse

We're skinless when we write, all nerves and need. To find the right people to read what we're writing — not to be overly dramatic here, but it's true — is fraught with danger. I make my students swear they won't let anyone outside the class read their work until at least the course is over. What we want to hear is: "This is fabulous, wonderful, timely, perfect, brilliant. *Don't change a word.*" It's more than likely that you will never hear all of this (especially the "don't change a word" part) in your whole writing career. But though you want praise and love and endless admiration, the important motive for having anyone read your stuff is to learn what's working and what's not, and how to make your work better. We need people who have no agenda with us yet have faith in us, who will validate what we're trying to do and let us know we're not wasting our time. People who know how to critique with generosity, honesty, and wisdom. We hand over a lot of power to these people, so choose your posse carefully.

For a long time now I've had my own validation squad, a small group of people I invite to see my works in progress. I trust them to look at my crudest, clumsiest noodlings and reward me with their candor.

— Twyla Tharp

19. The Five Characteristics of Good Writing

In a radio interview for one of my writing books, the interviewer asked me what the five characteristics of well-crafted writing were. Well, I didn't have a clue. My publisher's publicist had requested fifteen questions about the book that an interviewer could ask me (standard practice because interviewers rarely read the book), and in my own lazy moment I'd simply done a blog post asking my readers for questions, instead of writing them myself, then forwarded their questions on to the publicist. After all, I'd written the book. I knew all the answers, right? But I hadn't written about those five characteristics in my book, or if I had, I'd long forgotten them. So I bluffed my way through the interview. Later I went back to the fifteen questions and before the next interview wrote down answers to all the questions as if I were taking a test.

The point is that there are no cut-and-dried answers to questions about creative writing. Get a bunch of writers together, and you could come up with hundreds of characteristics of good writing.

But you might want to take another look at E. B. White's list of twenty-one reminders about style in chapter 5 of *The Elements of Style*. It's the most complete and eloquent writing lesson you'll ever have.

Do not overwrite. *Rich, ornate prose is hard to digest, generally unwholesome, and sometimes nauseating.*

— E. B. WHITE

20. Naked in the Hallway

I have a friend who has a large photograph of herself hanging in her downstairs hallway, and she's stark naked in it. There's also one of her husband. And these are not young people. The photographs were taken by a student from a nearby art college who wanted to photograph older people nude and who told my friend not to hold her stomach in, to just be herself. These are the bravest photographs I've ever seen, and beautiful too. Sure they reveal, well, everything, but — because of the lighting, the art involved — there's mystery to them.

I love to think of these photographs whenever I get all snarled up with the idea of exposing too much in my writing. As Tennessee Williams once said, "All good art is indiscretion."

I'm very relaxed about privacy because there is none left....John Perry Barlow, a former lyricist with the Grateful Dead...says the only way to have privacy [is to] expose it all and you have nothing to hide.

— LEONARD KLEINROCK

21. Finding the Spotlight

Jennifer Baszile, author of a memoir about growing up black in a white Los Angeles suburb, came to my class and told my students that before she could write her story, she had to own it. She had to know where the spotlight was and then stand in that light and give up the fear of people getting mad at her. She had to write her story as she had felt it so that her book could do its work in the world.

She was so beautiful and forceful and self-assured as she spoke to my class, no one could imagine her fearing what anyone thought. This is the kind of writer whose books you want to read and who, if possible, you want to hang out with — one who will let you know the struggle and the cost, not hide her fear.

Writing is a craft. You have to do the work, be willing to put scattered words down. The magic is in the commitment.

— JENNIFER BASZILE

22. A Writer's Lifestyle

In an interview Philip Roth, who lives alone in the country, said, "If I get up at five and I can't sleep and I want to work, I go out and go to work. So I work, I'm on call. I'm like a doctor and it's an emergency room. And I'm the emergency."

His ex-wife Claire Bloom wrote in her memoir about the time he asked her to describe what it was like to live in the country with a writer (he was working on a novel, and he wanted material for one of the characters). She was delighted to provide the material: "We don't go anywhere! We don't do anything! We don't see anyone!"

Writers do tend to be selfish and live exciting lives only in their heads. And they often think that their work is right up there in urgency and importance with the work of ER doctors. And sometimes you really need to think that way to get your work done.

Writers don't have lifestyles. They just sit in little rooms and write.
— Norman Mailer

23. What Writers Do

Nicholson Baker gets up at 4:00 AM without turning on the lights, sets his laptop screen to dark gray so he can't see the words, writes in the dark for a few hours, and then goes back to bed; he rises again at 8:30 to edit what he wrote. Orhan Pamuk writes by hand in notebooks of graph paper and leaves the opposite page blank for dialogue. Hilary Mantel tacks all her notes to a seven-foot-tall bulletin board in her kitchen. Colum McCann sometimes uses an eight-point font size that forces him to squint in order to read. Anne Rice uses fourteen-point Courier as a font. Allan Gurganus paces and reads his lines out loud. Cathleen Schine writes in her bed. Maya Angelou keeps a hotel room she writes in where there's a dictionary, a Bible, and a deck of playing cards on the bed and nothing on the walls. Anthony Trollope would write from 5:30 until 8:30 every morning with his watch in front of him. His self-imposed rule was to write 250 words every fifteen minutes.

What works, works.

Turn the ringer off on your phone. Don't answer the doorbell. Tell your loved ones that you cannot be disturbed. And if they cannot bear to live without you, go write in a coffee shop or library. Rent a room if you have to — just make the time to write your book.

— WALTER MOSLEY

24. Writing While Drooled Upon

I got really serious about writing when I was in my twenties and had two babies. I wrote at the kitchen table, I wrote while nursing, I wrote at an old dressing table in a bedroom, and later I wrote in a small sports car waiting for the kids to get out of school. I wrote with dogs drooling on me and with cats throwing up on my manuscripts. I wrote through not having enough money and my own guilt over not contributing anything to the household other than the clattering of my typewriter keys. Finally getting published wasn't due to strength of character or deep self-esteem; I wrote out of sheer stubbornness and panic. I didn't know if I was really a writer or simply a mother of small children who was going crazy in suburbia.

I think that a "real writer" is simply a person who keeps writing.

Of course if I were a real writer, predestined, dedicated, I'd work in the face of everything. . . . But as it is now I feel almost hysterical at the thought of concentration on one thing. I am never without interruption.

— M. F. K. FISHER

25. Failing Better

There's no clear path, no road without potholes, toward a piece of writing that says exactly what you mean to say in language that's clear and fresh. A couple of writers I know have a quote by Samuel Beckett about failing better hanging over their desks. My personal favorite failure quote is by Thomas Edison: "I didn't fail one thousand times. The lightbulb was an invention with one thousand steps."

What we need to do is think of all our failed drafts as simply steps toward the final one, the one that works.

Beckett had, tacked to the wall above his desk, a card on which were written the words: "Fail. Fail again. Fail better." It's a bad business, this writing. No marks on paper can ever measure up to the word's music in the mind, to the purity of the image before its ambush by language.

— MARY GORDON

26. The Trampoline as a Metaphor

"Do something every day that makes your hands sweat," says Carolyn See. I love this quote. But only in theory. Actually I prefer to be safe, calm, and to keep my dignity at all times; I don't want to lose my balance — inner or outer.

One day Emma, Axel, and Grace invited me onto their trampoline. I'm here to tell you that it is impossible to be calm and dignified on a trampoline. It is also impossible to feel safe on one. I crawled onto what looked like a big lake of black water and couldn't stand up. And these little kids, my grandchildren, none of whom were over four feet tall, were bouncing like Ping-Pong balls. I lay there just wanting the whole thing to be over, and then Emma grabbed me by the hand and said, "This is not scary! I'll hold your hand. We'll take baby steps." Very slowly I managed to get to my feet and then proceeded to inch across the trampoline in an upright position with Emma holding my hand. Then she instructed me to stand in one spot and to just bounce a bit. "It's okay if you fall down," she said, and I thought, *My God, she sounds just like me teaching a writing class.* And suddenly I realized the metaphor: there's no way to be any more dignified on a big piece of bouncing rubber than you are on a piece of paper. After I bounced a bit, I started to get the hang of it, and I began to jump. It was like flying. If you let go of how you look doing this, and aren't afraid to fall on your face, it's really fun. Kind of like writing.

Remember, it's a game. The objects are love, fun, and truth.
— Carolyn See

27. Fruitcakes and Discipline

Remember the joke about how there are only five fruitcakes in the world and they just keep getting sent back and forth around the world every Christmas? My mother used to make fruitcakes as presents, not the store-bought kind with neon-colored fruit but moist and dark and delicious, full of chopped nuts and raisins; she'd wrap them in bourbon-soaked cheesecloth from Thanksgiving until the holidays. The joke never fazed her. She just went on making those fruitcakes every year, and that's what everyone got as a present; and, unless they were lying, everyone loved them. She also practiced the piano every day of her life, and three weeks before she died, at age eighty-seven, she gave an hour-long recital of classical music at her retirement hotel.

Growing up, I had a number of problems with my mother. But now I often think of her dedication to the piano and her yearly fruitcakes, and I'm grateful for the example of discipline she set for me. Writing is just another version of practicing the piano and never giving up on fruitcakes.

We are what we repeatedly do. Excellence then, is not an act, but a habit.

— ARISTOTLE

28. In the Company of Animals

No wonder so many writers have animals. We're alone for most of our working day and would like some company, but we want company that won't talk to us.

There are cat-loving authors, most famously Colette. One of Marge Piercy's memoirs is entitled *Sleeping with Cats*. Bobbie Mason had a cat named Kiko, who she claimed was her chief inspiration. John Casey can write in a room with a cat but not a dog. "The cat doesn't want to pierce your attention barrier," he said.

But writers are also crazy about their dogs. Robin Romm's rescue dog named Mercy has shown up in her memoir and in at least three of her essays. Abigail Thomas and her three dogs appeared on the cover of one of her memoirs. Rick Bass, Barry Hannah, Jane Smiley, Denis Johnson, Ron Carlson, Armistead Maupin, Mark Doty, Pam Houston, Jon Katz, Susan Cheever, Ted Kooser — all have written about their dogs.

I used to have two cats, Stuart and Charlotte, who lived to be almost nineteen years old, and for all those years they were always on my desk, patient, calm, and looking as if they were channeling the muse for me. I now have a small rescue dog named Nelson who never lets me out of his sight and is more of a cheerleader than a muse. If I ask him who his favorite writer is, his ears go up and he hurls himself onto my lap, barking with great enthusiasm and adoration.

Molly the pit bull used to sit in the chair just behind me while I worked at my desk. She never commented on the writing, but since she loved everything I did, her presence did give me a sense of (unearned) security about it.

— BILLY MERNIT

29. First Things First

"Begin at the beginning and go on till you come to the end: then stop," says the king in *Alice's Adventures in Wonderland*.

John Irving writes his last sentence first.

Blaise Pascal said, "The last thing one discovers in writing a book is what to put in first."

Joyce Carol Oates says, "Only have faith: the first sentence can't be written until the last sentence has been written — only then do you know where you've been going, and where you've been."

When Jack Gilbert started out, he wouldn't write a poem until he knew the first line and the last.

I have a friend who fills dozens of notebooks before she actually begins writing a novel. Another simply jumps in and rewrites the first paragraph a hundred or so times. You can drive yourself crazy over how to start. Don't worry about it. *To start* is what's important.

I usually write the choruses first, because without a good chorus who gives a fuck?

— LADY GAGA

30. Out of the Box

Spalding Gray kept a cardboard box next to his desk, and he threw everything into it that was "unanswered, disturbing or relevant"; and then after a year or so he'd take everything out and try to put it together as a new monologue. "So I begin to have a new take on my life, on where I am historically," he said. "What I'm thinking about. How I'm interacting with people. It grows out of a series of anecdotes. Then I begin to see the common theme by speaking it."

Twyla Tharp has a cardboard file box too, and she fills it up with every item she uses in a new dance project. Everything that inspired her for the project — pieces of art, photos, research, CDs, news clippings, videos of the dancers working on the dance and of her working alone.

Sherman Alexie says, "My 'notebook' is actually a U-Haul cardboard box where I toss every scrap of paper I've ever touched with a pen, pencil, crayon, or typewriter: hotel stationery, paper, envelopes, etc. Drafts, story ideas, great themes I should be addressing, jokes."

My friend Jennie Nash uses five-dollar white plastic bins from Target when she starts writing a new novel because she thinks it's so much more powerful than opening a computer file or writing a project's name on a manila file tab; the bin is physical. "It defines a significant amount of space," she says.

On the other hand, Ray Bradbury thrives and creates in huge piles of paper that some people might call chaos.

Knowing that the box is always there gives me the freedom to venture out, be bold, dare to fall flat on my face. Before you can think out of the box, you have to start with a box.

— TWYLA THARP

31. Dreaming Your Ship

If you say your story is fiction, it's fiction. Period. How much or what part of it is autobiographical is nobody's business.

Sue Miller says, "The shaping, after all, is what it's all about. Every reader can sense the difference between a writer who embodies meaning through the events he describes and the writer who seems simply mired in those events." She prepares for the person in the third row who always asks how much of her novel is autobiographical by remembering a quote by John Cheever on the subject. Cheever compared the role autobiography played in fiction to that of reality in a dream. "As you dream your ship," he wrote, "you perhaps know the boat, but you're going toward a coast that's quite strange; you're wearing strange clothes, the language being spoken around you is a language you don't understand, but the woman on your left is your wife."

Sometimes I'm inclined to get cranky and bark about this: Give us writers a little credit, will you? We're not just keeping a diary here, we're inventing! Why can't you believe we're capable of making up a story from scratch? Of stringing together a long, elaborate lie, for heaven's sake?

— BARBARA KINGSOLVER

32. Improvisation

Everybody knows about actors doing improv — a line of dialogue, a situation, a word is thrown to actors, and they jump
into a scene. To an actor this is exhilarating. You don't think
— you just leap into the situation and start to feel and behave
and talk. Characters bloom, plots come out of thin air. It's very
much the same idea when you do quick writing exercises. It's
all improvisation. It's playing. Little kids do it all the time —
until someone tells them to calm down, and then they become
engineers or mathematicians or some other kind of grounded,
logical adult.

Think of jazz when you write. Write riffs. Play.

In improv there are no mistakes, only beautiful happy accidents.
— TINA FEY

33. Diving, Not Drowning

The fear of going back into your past — reliving trauma or grief — sometimes can block writing about the most important part of your story.

Carl Jung made the comparison of James Joyce and his daughter, who was schizophrenic, to two people in a river — the daughter was falling and could drown, but Joyce was diving.

To go back to pain is diving: cold, dangerous water and a swift current, but ultimately you're in charge of the dive and can return to the surface.

Writing it often wrings me out like a string mop. Some afternoons after I close my notebook — I'm working longhand — I just conk out on the floor of my study like a cross-country trucker.

— MARY KARR

34. The Duck or the Pâté?

"Wanting to meet an author because you like his work is like wanting to meet a duck because you like pâté."

Margaret Atwood has this epigram tacked to her bulletin board over her desk. She believes there are two entities who come under the label "the writer": the person who exists when no writing is going on — the one walking the dog, washing the car, etc. — and then the shadowy, slippery one who does the writing, the pâté. "And which half of the equation, if either, may be said to be authentic?" she asks.

If this idea gives you the slightest sense of freedom, you might think of isolating your writing self into a fearless, shadowy, and slippery wild person.

I do not know which of us has written this page.
— Jorge Luis Borges

35. Eight Ways to Sabotage Yourself

1. I have nothing original to write because everything interesting has already been written.
2. I don't have enough time right now. I'll start writing later. I'll write someday.
3. What if someone reads what I've written?
4. What if nobody reads what I've written?
5. I have to mow the lawn, clean the closets, wash the car, run a load of laundry *right now*.
6. I have to check my email.
7. I have to answer a few emails.
8. I have to check my Facebook page.

My personal favorite is email, though I'm also very big on cleaning closets and becoming domestic in a rather over-the-top, frightening way. Once in the middle of finishing a difficult novel that I had already accepted an advance for, I washed all the windows of my house and then started baking bread, loaf after loaf after loaf. Right now my favorite thing to avoid writing is to track orders I make online. I love to see what time things leave the warehouse, and the time is noted right down to the very second. I find this for some peculiar reason terribly interesting, and it also makes me feel hopeful and happy that there's such care and precision in this world.

The world is addictive. It wants us away from the desk, and a writer is a person who likes her work so much, that she's going to go get it. You've got to go upstream. It's against the tide to get this kind of work done.

— RON CARLSON

36. The Peculiar Art

In contrast with what most of the rest of the world does, writing is a peculiar sort of activity. Most other adults are out in the world, doing something of value: waiting tables, operating on gallbladders, running subways or flying planes, making bank loans, selling shoes, or anything that requires getting dressed and out of the house, being with other adults.

This is why I can't get enough of reading about other writers' rituals. I like to know that I'm not the only one feeling sloppy and slightly agoraphobic as I sit here in ancient yoga pants.

I'm not sure if it takes deep denial or courage to sit at one's desk day after day doing this. In the middle of my writing career, I once studied to go into a different profession; the main lure was having a desk out of the house and coworkers. Not to mention a regular paycheck. I studied for two years and had a good time doing this job, but I couldn't get over the sense of not being in my own skin and had to quit.

It seems odd, even insane, to be locked away in a room, trying to hammer words into their correct places. I often have intense longings to go to an office — in order to share the burdens of my work with other people, as workers in offices can.

— ALAIN DE BOTTON

37. Being a Writer

When I was in third grade, a writer came to speak at school assembly, and it was the first time that I realized, truly understood, that real people wrote books. It suddenly seemed a very accessible thing to do. If you loved stories, you could become something called *a writer* and make them up yourself.

When Richard Ford was a little boy growing up in Jackson, Mississippi, his mother told him that a writer lived across the street and her name was Eudora Welty. Though Ford didn't meet her for years, he said living near her and being around her made it clear to him that being a writer was okay and worthwhile.

Oh, I didn't know I was going to write the kind of thing I've written, but I knew I was going to write — I just had to....I can't remember a time I didn't make up stories. I don't think I called it writing.

— ALICE MUNRO

38. Ideal Conditions

Conditions most likely will be not only un-ideal — but actively against sitting down to write. There will be the ping of email arrival, the phone ringing, any number of family emergencies, food to be bought or cooked, things leaking or smoking or disappearing that have to be dealt with. Children or pets with immediate needs. You will never, ever find time; you just have to make it.

Or the paradox — you can have too much quiet, too much time. Hours and days and months of time and opportunity. Oddly this too can be so overwhelming that it makes writing difficult.

Carol Shields began writing in fits and starts when she had five babies in one decade. When they were all in school, she was able to write two pages a day, and finished her first novel in nine months. (Just like another baby.) She never wrote that quickly again and said in an interview, "It's funny, because now I have the whole day and my output is no more than it was then."

Either way — with no time or too much time — decide how long you'll write. Fifteen minutes? An hour? All morning? Until 3:30 in the afternoon? Decide and then do it.

A writer who waits for ideal conditions under which to work will die without putting a word on paper.

— E. B. WHITE

39. Keeping a Journal

You have a notebook, right? An inexpensive spiral lined note-book, or a special computer file, or one of those beautiful journal books (which can be intimidating), or a big envelope full of scraps of paper. This diary, or notebook, or journal, or big envelope, whatever it is, is simply your practice space. Don't overthink it. Just write in it — hourly, daily, or once a week. Whatever works for you.

If you were an artist, you'd have a sketch pad. Or if you played the flute, you'd sit around endlessly practicing. Or if you were a serious dancer, you'd be going to class every day. Writers take notes about what they think, feel, imagine, and experience. It's that simple.

The writer's life is so oddly splintered/isolated and internal most of the time, with moments of intense self-exposure. I think of the journal as a witness, a repository and playground. It is where I begin things or bring thoughts to some kind of clarity.

— DOROTHY ALLISON

40. Inspiration

One of the definitions of the word *inspiration* is "the drawing of air into the lungs."

Every once in a while just take a deep breath. Relax your shoulders. Exhale.

I don't know anything about inspiration, because I don't know what inspiration is — I've heard about it, but I never saw it.
— WILLIAM FAULKNER

41. Overnight Success Story

Years ago, as a totally green and naive nineteen-year-old actress, I had the luck to be cast with Ruth Gordon in a Broadway play directed by her husband, Garson Kanin. Ruth was in her midsixties then and not only a Broadway star but also a successful playwright, screenwriter, and author of several memoirs. She worked harder than anyone I had ever known. She never took a performance for granted, never coasted through; it was all about hard work and pushing herself to be better. Before every single performance she'd be the first to arrive at the theater; she'd go to her dressing room and go over her part, line by line. Six years later, in her seventies, she became a movie star. She won the Academy Award and Golden Globe for *Rosemary's Baby*, another Golden Globe for *Inside Daisy Clover*, and, as Maude, helped make *Harold and Maude* into a classic film.

Pan me, don't give me the part, publish everybody's book but this one and I will still make it!

— RUTH GORDON

42. Darling, What If You Tried...

Ruth Gordon's husband, Garson Kanin, was the master of critique. During rehearsals he'd push you to work harder by using the most positive words and most respectful attitude. How interesting you were, what clever business you came up with for that scene, what a good actor you were. And then with great respect he'd say, "But darling, what if you tried..." And then you tried what he suggested, and everything changed and got much better.

This also works if you're in a writing workshop giving feedback to your fellow writers.

And sometimes with small children.

I'm still learning from the example of these mentors, and from others, past and present.

— JAY PARINI

43. Nelson's News

Every morning Nelson, my stalwart rescue dog, flies down the stairs from the bedroom to the kitchen, eats the same exact breakfast with total delight and appreciation, then walks and runs three or four miles with me on the beach. His legs are about eight inches high; I figure every one of my steps is worth six of his, so he's actually covering twenty-some miles every morning.

He treats everything — sand, bike path, bushes, even the wind — like his very own morning newspaper. His sense of smell is one thousand times greater than mine, and he can hear much higher and lower sounds than I can. Not only can he smell and hear better; he's always alert, like a canine cop. I walk around in my human fog, lost in my own head, while he comes up with twenty-two words for *seagull*.

All perception is limited.... What we take in is a partial rendering of the world. To go for a walk with a dog is enough to illustrate this principle.

— MARK DOTY

44. Sad Flailing and Panic

Mary Roach, who has written some of the most riveting, funny nonfiction you'll ever want to read, describes her writing process as "utter confusion for three or four months and no sense of what the book will be." I love reading this. I love hearing about her "low-grade panic" and her "sad flailing." If Mary Roach feels like this, it somehow legitimizes my own panic and flailing.

I love it when Joy Williams says, "Whenever the writer writes, it's always three o'clock in the morning." And when Stephen King tells us "there came a point when I couldn't write any longer because I didn't know what to write.... I wasn't the first writer to discover this awful place, and I'm a long way from being the last; this is the land of writer's block." (Stephen King with writer's block!)

But I also love it when he tells us that writing is magic.

Writing is magic, as much the water of life as any other creative art. The water is free. So drink. Drink and be filled up.

— STEPHEN KING

45. Stubborn and Stupid

At nineteen, when I told my father I was quitting college to go to New York to become an actress, he told me I was so stubborn and stupid that I'd probably make it. Friends are shocked when I tell them my father called me stubborn and stupid, but even though we were having a big fight when he said this, I understood that he meant it with love. I was stubborn, as stubborn as he was, and I was stupid in the sense that I was unfazed by the fact that thousands of other nineteen-year-old girls were storming Broadway and Hollywood to become actresses.

Being stubborn can be as important as talent, if not more so. And sometimes being a little stupid about the competition isn't a bad thing, either.

A certain amount of stubbornness — pigheadedness — is essential.
— MADELEINE L'ENGLE

46. Frou-Frou in Your Head

It's all frou-frou — the dreams, the fantasies of writing, of publishing poems or books or essays; it's all just a lot of wishing — unless you write something down.

Remember this: there is nothing until there's something on the page.

To get started I will accept anything that occurs to me. Something always occurs, of course, to any of us. We can't keep from thinking.
— WILLIAM STAFFORD

47. The Writer's Club

One of my students wrote an essay about losing weight and how she then realized that a "thin club" existed because people started treating her differently when she was thin. This got me to thinking about clubs, how we're all more or less organized into clubs that are not that different from those in high school — the popular kids, jocks, nerds, weirdos, etc.

But things do change when we grow up, and some of us weirdos now belong to the coolest club of all, the Writer's Club. We get to dress any way we please, we get to keep our own hours, we can act a little odd and silent (people will think we're taking notes in our head). The only condition of membership is that we have to write. Because once you stop writing, you get kicked out.

I didn't start writing until I was forty-seven. I had always wanted to write but thought you needed a degree, or membership in a club nobody had asked me to join.... It was a long time before I realized that you don't have to start right, you just have to start.

— ABIGAIL THOMAS

48. Community

Obviously some people believe that writing can be taught — witness the vast number of MFA creative writing programs, let alone the number of writing courses offered. Joanna Trollope says that she's always "faintly fussed" by the idea of these courses. She believes that in a class you can learn how to structure a novel, do pace and tension, and create dialogue, but you can't learn what she calls the right kind of observation.

John Irving says, "This is what I can 'teach' a young writer: something he'll know for himself in a little while longer; but why wait to know these things? I am talking about technical things, the only things you can presume to teach, anyway."

One of the most important things a course or a workshop can do is offer a community for writers. The real world looks at writing (unless you're making a phenomenal amount of money at it) as a slightly suspect activity. A little self-indulgent, a bit pie-in-the-sky. A class offers you a group of people who share your passion and take that pie very seriously.

Finding community with other writers is as necessary and as important as cultivating writerly solitude in a room of one's own.
— JULIE CHECKOWAY

49. Tilting

"Being yourself in a role, but tilted."
— DUSTIN HOFFMAN

I copied this down when Dustin Hoffman was interviewed at Actors Studio on television a few years ago, and it recently surfaced on a little scrap of paper in my office.

I love the idea of acting, or writing, coming from a "tilted" part of us. Writing from a perspective that's honest yet emphasizing certain traits. This is so true; if you're writing fiction, you may find that there's a tilted part of you in all your characters. Or you turn yourself into a character when you're writing personal nonfiction no matter how honest you're striving to be.

I have a talented and witty student whose writing sometimes veers off into the sensitive and emotional. But that isn't his best voice or, oddly enough, the one that rings most true. He is a person of deep feeling and sensitivity, but the part of him that works best for the memoir he's writing is the tilted, tougher, and funnier part of his character.

Style is knowing who you are, what you want to say, and not giving a damn.

— GORE VIDAL

50. The Narrative of Your Life

Gabriel Byrne in an interview talked about his role as a psychoanalyst in *In Treatment* and his fascination with how therapy can help you recognize the real narrative of your life and come to terms with it. How in ordinary life, he said, "we have a tendency…to kind of magnify certain things and give them an importance, idealize certain things, and be in denial about other things."

This seems very close to writing the narrative of our life on the page — and the need to come to terms with it. Sure we tilt ourselves as characters in our own stories, but unless we turn to fiction, we're on the path to finding our true selves through writing.

First we wrap our lives in language and then we act on who we say we are. We proceed from the word into the world and make a world based on our stories.

— CHRISTINA BALDWIN

51. Nothing New under the Sun

A student who writes wonderfully funny stuff about families and growing older emailed me that she had read Nora Ephron's latest book and that Nora had hijacked the subjects she herself was going to write about. I emailed her back (in caps so she'd pay attention): "ALL OUR BEST MATERIAL HAS ALREADY BEEN COVERED BY WONDERFUL WRITERS. IF WE LET THAT STOP US, NOTHING NEW WOULD EVER GET WRITTEN."

Everything has been said; but not everything has been said superbly, and even if it had been, everything must be said freshly, over and over.

— PAUL HORGAN

52. The Writer as Spy

Eavesdropping is a constant source of fresh writing prompts. Because I'm out walking and running on the beach every morning, I hear fragments of intimate conversations all the time as people run, walk, skate, or bike by. Snatches of dialogue: "Well, of course everyone else was really laughing, but she was so damn intense because…" I continue on, wondering why she, whoever she is, was so intense, why everyone was "of course" laughing. Once I heard a woman say to two guys she was walking with, "I had this really bad breakup, so I started writing."

The great advantage of being a writer is that you can spy on people. You're there, listening to every word, but part of you is observing. Everything is useful to a writer, you see — every scrap, even the longest and most boring of luncheon parties.

— Graham Greene

53. On Work and Sentences

When asked where his discipline comes from, John Banville said that he's an essentially religious type and that about the time he gave up Catholicism in his teens, he began to write. "It is a great privilege to make one's living from writing sentences," he says. "The sentence is the greatest invention of civilization. To sit all day long assembling these extraordinary strings of words is a marvelous thing. I couldn't ask for anything better. It's as near to godliness as I can get."

Annie Proulx connected her love of writing a good sentence to her rural upbringing. "There is difficulty involved in going from the basic sentence that's headed in the right direction to making a fine sentence," she says. "But it's a joyous task. It's hard, but it's joyous. Being raised rural, I think work is its own satisfaction. It's not seen as onerous, or a dreadful fate. It's like building a mill or a bridge or sewing a fine garment or chopping wood — there's a pleasure in constructing something that really works."

When I begin a novel I don't want to be thinking about When does Nancy see Fred again? *I know when Nancy sees Fred again. All I want to be thinking about is,* How good is this sentence? Was it long? Should it be followed by another long one? Should it be followed then by another short one? *That's all I want to be thinking about.*

— JOHN IRVING

54. The Beginning Writer

In the middle of an all-day workshop that I was teaching, one of the participants, who had told us during introductions that she had a PhD, came up to me at the break and said, "Well, I almost walked out when you started talking. I was on my feet. I was out the door." When I asked her why, she said, "I was afraid this was going to be just a beginner's workshop!"

Earlier in the morning I had talked about how fearful most people are about writing, and quoted a poll about what people feared more than death — public speaking and writing. "I talk that way to all my classes, beginning and advanced," I said to the woman. "We're all beginners when we write." I don't think she believed me. But it was the truth. We're all beginners when we look at the blank page to fill.

It's a very excruciating life facing that blank piece of paper every day and having to reach up somewhere into the clouds and bring something down out of them.

— TRUMAN CAPOTE

55. One Lie Leads to Another

My most embarrassing moment as a child was telling a huge lie in show-and-tell in first grade that spread through the entire school. (I told my class that I had famous movie star siblings.) I learned early on that one lie requires a series of subsequent lies, a whole structure of lies, to support it. Kind of like writing fiction.

A writer is congenitally unable to tell the truth and that is why we call what he writes fiction.

— WILLIAM FAULKNER

56. No Drama

Flannery O'Connor once said, "Every morning between 9 and 12 I go to my room and sit before a piece of paper. Many times, I just sit for three hours with no ideas coming to me. But I know one thing. If an idea does come between 9 and 12, I am there ready for it."

My writing teacher quoted this to our class years ago, and I never forgot it. It speaks so quietly to the whole business of inspiration that it lets the air out of the drama of writing, the specialness of it. Because there is no drama — it's just you sitting there in a room, and maybe you get an idea, maybe not. But in any event you sit there.

Inspiration is to work every day.

— Charles Baudelaire

57. Juggling

Unless you live alone and have devoted servants and assistants taking care of all the routine details of your life, you bounce from going to the bank, taking kids to school or parents to doctors, grocery shopping, car maintenance, haircuts, folding laundry, etc., to the world you're creating, or re-creating, on paper. Not to mention working at your day job too. This transition is not always smooth and decorous. It can make you insane. It can make you want to give up writing. Or give yourself the grand excuse of waiting to write until you get organized and everything settles down.

But few writers have personal assistants or servants, and most have day jobs. All my writer friends teach. Ted Kooser and Wallace Stevens worked as insurance executives, Anton Chekhov and William Carlos Williams were part of a long tradition of doctor-writers, Scott Turow still practices law, Shirley Jackson had six children, and David Sedaris cleaned houses and, as we all know, worked at Macy's as a Christmas elf.

So in the end you don't go crazy. And you don't give up writing. You juggle, just like everybody else.

I have spent so long erecting partitions around the part of me that writes — learning how to close the door on it when ordinary life intervenes, how to close the door on ordinary life when it's time to start writing again — that I'm not sure I could fit the two parts of me back together now.

— ANNE TYLER

58. Retreating to Play

While driving up to the mountains to conduct a writer's retreat, I hear a commercial on the radio, something about health — how we all need to play to be healthier, but as we grow up, gathering information takes precedence over being creative, and we stop playing.

It's the perfect opening idea for a writer's retreat — let's play! Ideally, at a retreat you let go of outside information; you listen to yourself. You let go of what you should know, need to learn. You play.

I once did writing workshops in an elementary school, and it was the kindergarteners and kids in the early grades who knew how to play with words. "A horn sounds red!" one wrote. "Mad is like touching the devil," wrote another. "Mad is so bad it tastes like liver." By the time they got to third grade, they were obsessing about whether to write their names in the upper left-hand or right-hand corner of the page.

It takes a long time to become young.

— Picasso

59. What Writers Can Learn from Six-Year-Olds

Here's what I learned from babysitting Emma for a week when she was six years old:

CREATIVITY. Use any and all opportunities to be creative. (She pulls up my sweater and writes on my back with a ballpoint pen — "BABS LOVES EMMA" surrounded with flowers — as I attempt to sound professional on a phone call.)

ENERGY. You need to practice, and you need energy to do the work you love. (She dances *nonstop* as we watch DVDs of *Singing in the Rain* and *Funny Face*.)

EMOTION AND PASSION. You can't write about emotions unless you're in touch with your own feelings. (She goes from tears and sobs — "You can't kill fruit flies! They're part of nature!" — to laughter and wild joy *in seconds*.)

FOCUS. Concentrate on what you love, ignoring what people think you should do. (She plays with a huge plastic purple airplane filled with things called Polly Pocket People and then distributes the PPP all over the house.)

CURIOSITY. Question every aspect of life. ("What makes an ocean?" she asks. "How do you get a heart attack?" "How many husbands have you had?")

I am compelled to write about this even though it embarrasses me to keep talking about my grandchildren. Still, this is supposed to be a writer's journal, and if there's one thing I've learned about writing it is to follow your compulsions.

— ELLEN GILCHRIST

60. Showing Up

Let's say that you've set a time to write. Your muse, inspiration, your heart, whatever you want to call that spark you need to connect to, waits. And then you decide to do something else, or the idea of going to your desk to write whatever you need to write suddenly scares the daylights out of you.

Mary Oliver writes about what would have happened with Romeo and Juliet if they'd made appointments to meet and then didn't show up: "One or the other lagging, or afraid, or busy elsewhere — there would have been no romance, no passion." She uses this as a metaphor for making an appointment with yourself to write and then not showing up. "If you are reliably there, it begins to show itself — soon it begins to arrive when you do." But if you're not reliable, it may show up only briefly or not at all. "Why should it?" she asks. "It can wait. It can stay silent a lifetime."

Don't silence your heart. Make a date and show up.

Now this is very important, and can hardly be emphasized too strongly: you have decided to write at four o'clock, and at four o'clock you must! No excuses can be given.

— DOROTHEA BRANDE

61. Writing Hours

Tennessee Williams wrote every day from 6:00 AM until noon up until the very end of his life. In her early career, Marguerite Young wrote from 8:00 AM to 5:00 PM; then when she got older, she began a few hours later. Jack Kerouac wrote from midnight until dawn, and when he got tired, he had a drink. Julian Barnes writes between 10:00 AM and 1:00 PM and works seven days a week. "Weekends are good working time because people think you've gone away and don't disturb you," he says. "So is Christmas. Everyone's out and no one phones. I always work on Christmas morning — it's a ritual."

And then there's Téa Obreht, who was finishing graduate school and teaching when she began work on her first novel, which would become a bestseller when she was twenty-five years old. While working on the book, she didn't have enough time in the day to write, so she wrote at night — from 10:00 PM until 4:00 AM.

I'd write through the night, teach and then go to sleep, write through the night, teach and go to sleep....It's not very healthy. It's dark out, and you don't get to see a lot of people.

— TÉA OBREHT

62. Feast or Famine: Part 1

A student was lamenting that he had too much story for his memoir. He said there was the Mormon part and coming out of the closet, then the time in Hawaii and drug addiction, and then the hospital and getting clean and sober, and now the leather clubs. I told him it all sounded like great material for a memoir.

"But there are too many stories!" he said.

Another writer at a retreat had told me the same thing. "There's just too much to write about!" she said.

This overabundance of material can also be called standing in your own way. If there's too much to write about, you can just throw up your hands and say the hell with it. Or you can start writing those stories one page at a time.

Oh yes, I can write! I mean I've a fizz of ideas. What I dread is bottling them to order.

— VIRGINIA WOOLF

63. Feast or Famine: Part 2

The famine is the stuck part, when you suddenly believe there is not one interesting thing that has ever happened to you in your entire life. This feeling will pass. Don't worry about it. Get out your journal and whine for a few pages.

We're all living the first draft of our lives.

— CAROLYN SEE

64. Writing Is Not Pretty

Every once in a while a student will ask me why I don't do the writing exercises with the class. The reason is simple: when I write, I'm selfish. When I teach, I focus on my students; I love their stories, their courage to sit there and write on demand, their curiosity and enthusiasm, their respect for and kindness to each other. When teaching, I'm a fairly generous and accessible person, but put a pen in my hand, give me a writing prompt, and I'll revert to my selfish, obsessed, agoraphobic writing self.

When you write, you write. It's not always pretty, but I don't know any other way to get work done. So, get selfish, haul in the drawbridge, and give all your energy to your writing.

All writers are vain, selfish and lazy, and at the very bottom of their motives lies a mystery. Writing a book is a long, exhausting struggle, like a long bout of some painful illness. One would never undertake such a thing if one were not driven by some demon whom one can neither resist nor understand.

— GEORGE ORWELL

65. Why You Don't Show Your Work to Your Spouse

When Norris Church Mailer showed her husband, Norman Mailer, the first one hundred pages of a novel she was working on, he said, "It's not as bad as I thought it would be."

Apparently she did not shoot him or leave him; she just put the pages away for a while. Later she went on to finish the novel and got it published. Then she wrote a sequel and got that published too.

The goal is paramount. One's mate is present, therefore, as an effective and useful aide-de-camp or as an impediment.

— NORMAN MAILER

66. The Pitfalls of Grammar

Emma, at age seven, came to my house with her homework folder full of assignments that made me remember why I had done so badly in school. But also included were instructions for writing a story. There were writing prompts — good. But also rules that struck me as a little scary. I realized why most of us have so many hang-ups about writing — indentation was very important, punctuation, spelling, and there had to be at least eight sentences.

Emma chose the writing prompt "This Halloween..." After about the third sentence of what she was doing that Halloween, she ground to a halt. I suggested she might pretend that it was about the cats. Costumes for cats? "Cats craving candy!" she yelled. "Wonderful!" I said. She started to write. Then clutched her head. "Oh no, I spelled *making* wrong. I wrote 'meking'!" I told her not to worry about spelling. "I have to indent!" she said. "We're not supposed to use the word *fun*!" She was erasing like mad. I told her all the stuff I tell my adult students: let it be sloppy and messy, don't worry about punctuation and spelling, this is the creative part, you can always come back to it and edit. She looked at me. "You know how you can tell when you have eight sentences? You count the periods."

Lose control. Don't think. Don't get logical.

— Natalie Goldberg

67. Seinfeld's Calendar

As a guy jogging on the beach passed me, he said to his friend, "You just sit down every day and fucking do it."

Yes!

Or was he talking about paying his bills? Doing homework, taxes? Whatever he meant, I like to think he was going to sit down to write every day.

When Jerry Seinfeld started out as a comic, he wrote jokes every day. To motivate himself he hung up a big wall calendar that showed a whole year, and bought a red pen. Every day that he wrote a joke he marked a red *X* over the day. After a few days of this he had a chain of red *X*s. He figured his job was to keep that chain going.

I didn't express confidence so much as blind faith that if you go in and work every day it will get better. Three days will go by and you will be in that office and you will think every day is terrible. But on the fourth day, if you do go in, if you don't go into town or out in the garden, something usually will break through.

— JOAN DIDION

68. Making Use of Fear

Dennis Palumbo writes about sitting on a ledge a thousand feet up, shaking with fear, after he climbed the Grand Teton in Wyoming. He told his climbing instructor he was afraid, and the instructor replied, "Good. Otherwise I wouldn't climb with you. Fear keeps you in the here-and-now."

When I was an actress, the day before opening night on Broadway, I would be so terrified, so overwhelmed with stage fright, that I'd have fantasies that maybe the theater would catch fire and the performance would be canceled, or maybe I'd be hit by a bus and have to go to the hospital. But fear is also energy; climbing up a steep mountain peak, going out on stage for two hours in front of an audience, or writing a book — none of this works if you're laid-back and casual about the whole thing. A la-di-da attitude doesn't help you up a mountain, rivet an audience, or get you to the last page of your book.

In that space between my heart and diaphragm was the fear I always feel before writing, when my soul is poised to leap alone.
— ANDRE DUBUS

69. Your Naked Prose

Writing is so intensely personal — our thoughts, emotions, memories, imagination, fantasies right out there under the spotlight — that it really is a striptease act. So it's natural to panic if someone doesn't think your naked prose is perfect. Hopefully when you get feedback, you can use it to make your work better. But if someone gives self-serving, snarky comments in a workshop or writing group to build up his or her own ego, leave at the first opportunity. Find a more positive and generous group of people whose comments concern your intention, not their expectations. You can't feel free to write your best if you sense the knives are being sharpened behind your back.

Every word she writes is a lie, including "and" and "the."

— MARY MCCARTHY
(being snarky about Lillian Hellman)

70. The Right Age to Write

In the comment section of my blog, a reader once asked if age thirty-five was too old to start writing. A fifty-year-old chimed in that he was agonizing over the same question. This started a whole slew of comments from people obsessing on the age issue.

Too old to write means what? Perhaps you are too old to take up skydiving or to try rodeo roping. But why would you be too old to write? If you can hold a pen, use a computer, or even just dictate, you aren't too old to write.

Norman Maclean wrote his first novel, *A River Runs through It*, when he was in his seventies. It became a literary classic as well as a Robert Redford film.

Harry Bernstein struggled to become a writer all his life and finally received critical acclaim and literary fame when his first memoir about his childhood, *The Invisible Wall*, was published when he was ninety-six years old. *Publishers Weekly* gave it a starred review. He published a second memoir a year later, when he was ninety-seven.

The first 25 years of my life are something I would rather forget, but the contrary has taken place. The older I get the more alive those years have become.

— HARRY BERNSTEIN

71. Being Your Own Shrink

You can be your own shrink in your journal, but this can be dicey to pull off when you're trying to write a book. When I went through a divorce, I was too crazy and angry to write anything except morning/noon/evening rants in my journal. A year later I gave some of my divorce to a character in a novel, but I still didn't have the distance that it took to shape things into fiction. And I never did pull that novel off. Finally — taking more time than I care to tell you — I wrote and published a long essay about the beginning and end of my twenty-six-year first marriage. I finally had some perspective, but it took time.

You have to have done that hard psychological work before you sit down to write.

— MARY KARR

72. Writer's Remorse

The long essay I finally wrote about my first marriage turned out well; enough time had passed that I could find humor in events that had at one point made me insane. The essay was very personal, it acknowledged the love that had been in the marriage and the pain and bad behavior when it unraveled, and the ending was slightly snide. But by the time the essay was published in an anthology, I'd just had a nice lunch with my ex-husband. We share beautiful daughters and grandchildren, we've become good friends, and I wanted to keep the peace. I was scheduled to read the essay at an event later that week that was going to be recorded for YouTube, and I decided I didn't want to make the essay any more public than it already was. I just couldn't read it. But then I thought, well, that's where I was when I wrote it, it's my view and truth, and if you start editing yourself to keep the peace, you'll end up with nothing in print.

This is something I've told my students over and over for years and years. Sometimes you teach what you need to learn.

To write was to court overwhelming feeling. Not to write was to avoid. . . . And so I'd write, when I could, recording what approached like someone in a slow-moving but unstoppable accident, who must look and look away at once.

— MARK DOTY

73. Starting Again and Again

I started writing stories at age six, the only time writing felt really easy and great fun. I wrote some ghastly poems and angst-filled stories as a teenager, and though not exceptionally bright, I did have the smarts to realize that it was easier to act than to write. So I became an actress. But ten years later I was back at it, trying to write, going nowhere, starting and stopping. Finally, in my early thirties I took a creative writing course at a community college and ever since then — though there may have been blocks huge enough to stop trucks, and swarms of rejections — writing has been simply part of who I am and what I do.

But there are always starts — a new essay, a new chapter, a new book. If you're a writer, each blank page can be a new start; and it never gets any easier.

Is starting hard? You know it. I don't know what you do when you start, but I clean my desk.... I make a lot of stupid appointments that I make sound important.... Avoidance, delay, denial.... I'm always scared that I'm not gonna know what to do. It's a terrifying moment.

— FRANK GEHRY

74. The Truth and Nothing But

In an interview John Rechy was asked if a certain scene he'd written in his memoir had actually happened, and he said, "No! But it should have happened. And so, because it should have happened, here it does."

I was once on a panel of writers that nearly came to blows on the subject of whether absolute truth is needed in nonfiction. One writer said she had left out three siblings in a memoir she'd written; another gave a short, impassioned speech on literature having no boundaries. The rest of us believed that if you pop a nonfiction label on what you write, be it memoir or essay, the reader is going to take it as the truth, and that's what it's got to be, to the best of your ability. Sure, you might guess about the color of a shirt you wore that day or whether the eggs were fried or scrambled, but if that shirt felt red in your memory, and if you suddenly can see those eggs scrambled, so be it. Go with your best guess. But if you want to get rid of some sisters or brothers, or write what should have happened, I think you might consider calling it fiction.

The writer of memoir makes a pact with her reader that what she writes is the truth as best she can tell it. But the original pact, the real deal, is with herself. Be honest, dig deep, or don't bother.

— Abigail Thomas

75. Signs and Messages from Above

I believe in signs. I'm not sure if they come from angels or God or Jesus or Buddha or whoever or whatever — but they're messages pointing in the right direction, and we can pay attention or not. I have an email taped to the wall over my computer from a woman who read one of my long-out-of-print novels ten times and asked when I was going to publish another one. Her email arrived on a day when I was in despair, clutching my head over a new novel I was trying to write.

Once my friend Billy and I were walking on the beach, and he was telling me the plot for his new novel. Suddenly there was this amazing rainbow overhead. A rainbow! Talk about messages. It was pretty impressive.

So watch for signs to continue writing. And ignore all negative messages.

I stood, alone, and the world swayed. I am a fugitive and a vagabond, a sojourner seeking signs.

— ANNIE DILLARD

76. Writers Gnashing Teeth

My dentist told me that I'm wearing down my teeth by grinding them. I told him I didn't grind them. "I have a lot of patients who are writers," he said. "They all grind their teeth."

[Dr.] Stevens is backing two of my upper jaw incisors with gold; otherwise, he says, they will grind themselves down and crack up.
— CHRISTOPHER ISHERWOOD

77. Why Write?

I mean, really, why write? Why not go back to school or do good works or raise chickens or focus on your job or plant tomatoes? Why put yourself through this?

In her poem "The Summer Day," Mary Oliver writes about paying attention, kneeling in the grass to observe a grasshopper, her realization of how short life is. The final lines of the poem ask the reader: "Tell me, what is it you plan to do / with your one wild and precious life?"

Perhaps this is why you write. This is what you need to do with your one wild and precious life.

You were made and set here to give voice to this, your own astonishment.

— Annie Dillard

78. Dimes in Ivory Soap

You're the only one who remembers what it was like to have breakfast — or not have breakfast — with your family. You're the only one who can describe your first kiss, how you felt when your parents got you a dog (or wouldn't get you a dog), your favorite shoes as a kid, the games you played, the music you listened to, the family jokes, or lack of jokes. If you don't write down your past, it's gone.

When my brother was six years old, he got the idea of cutting into bars of Ivory soap and inserting dimes. I cannot tell you how excited and mystified I was when I discovered my first dime while taking a bath one day. Even my parents were puzzled and fascinated by the mystery of the Ivory soap dimes. My brother, who eventually confessed to the dimes, also painted our cat's tail orange when he was three years old. Our parents are gone now, so only my brother and I know these stories. And now so do you because I wrote them down.

I am the only one who can tell the story of my life and say what it means.

— DOROTHY ALLISON

79. What Does Your Mother Think?

When I have guest speakers in my class who have written memoirs, one of the first things my students ask is, "What did your mother say when she read it?"

But what about mothers writing about their children? My kids have some pretty amazing material, but that's one privacy line I won't cross in my writing. I'll write about them — the funny stuff — but I won't steal the heavy moments in their lives.

Though just recently, as I was discussing this with a daughter, she said in a dark tone, "Remember writing about the Snickers bars under Gillan's bed?" I asked her what on earth she was talking about. "You wrote a poem about her messy bedroom," she said, "and then read it to her class."

The thing about being a writer is that you just learn to live with your guilt.

I never once encountered a student who didn't worry, at some level, that a friend or family member was going to be violated, punished or crucified in a piece of writing. (Mothers take an exceptionally heavy rap with younger students.) ... And it often afflicted young writers with classic writer's block before they'd written so much as a single word.

— Carol Shields

80. The Strip Club

Maud Casey wrote in an essay that she felt as if she were chasing her parents' shadows through the novels they wrote. "There they were, flitting up ahead on the next page. And when I read the books they had written, it was as though I had walked into the strip club of their imaginations."

Ah, the strip club of our imaginations being read by our children! There's a thought to stop you dead in your tracks. And if you don't have children, you might find something else to stop you. Your parents, maybe.

Maud Casey goes on to write that her parents gave her a profound gift — restless discontent. And she says this restless discontent led her to "the solitary turning inward required to write."

Everyone looks in his own way for something that will cure the silence, the feeling of guilt, the feeling of panic.

— Natalia Ginzburg

81. Writing on Water

People always ask writers what they write with. Most write on computers because work sent out needs to be pristine on the page, but I think I wrote better on a typewriter using carbon paper for copies and Wite-Out for typos. With no Delete button to constantly edit myself, I had to think more, try harder. And I loved the loud clacketing sound a typewriter made. People *knew* I was working.

Annie Dillard in an interview once ranted that computers can create huge mushrooming paragraphs. Sometimes with these computer keys I feel like I'm doodling on a piano or writing on water. It's too easy to revise, to slash and burn without letting the writing cool, or even worse, to blither on and on into lethal mushroom clouds of words.

There was a pleasant rhythm to those hard-typing times, during which I would neatly stack up 10 to 12 finished pages daily, the whole business accumulating in a very satisfying way.

— T. C. BOYLE

82. Finding a Genre

I don't really know how you find your own genre. I often say to my students that what you love to read is what you'll love to write, but luck and timing are involved too; it's like falling in love. Personally, I'm promiscuous; I loved writing fiction, and then I took up poetry, and next I fell into children's stories, and then fooled around with essays, and now I'm involved with nonfiction books.

Samuel Beckett referred to finding a genre as needing "to find a form that accommodates the mess."

Now, I want the easiness of poetry. The brevity of the poem....No more plotting any more plots.

— MAXINE HONG KINGSTON

83. Retyping the Best

When Donald Ray Pollock turned forty-five, he decided he wanted to do something different with his life; he was going to learn how to write. He began by retyping stories by writers he liked — John Cheever, Richard Yates, and Ernest Hemingway — and then he'd carry the stories around with him, reading and rereading them. "I'm not a real close reader," he said, "and typing those stories out gave me the chance to see this is how you make a transition, this is how you do dialogue."

I once read about a writing teacher in the 1950s who used to make her students (some of whom became famous) type out whole published novels by their favorite writers. One of the reasons she had them do this was to make them realize how long it takes just to *type* a whole book, let alone dream it up and write many drafts.

When I got reprint rights for an essay for an anthology I was editing, I had to retype the essay from the original book into my manuscript. The author was one of my favorite writers, and it was an eerie and intimate experience to type out her sentences.

I'm probably the least cerebral guy you're ever going to meet as a writer. I just keep knocking away until something comes.

— DONALD RAY POLLOCK

84. How to Be a Writer

"Make a place to sit down," reads the first line of Wendell Berry's poem "How to Be a Poet." The second line is: "Sit down. Be quiet." The poem is so simple and deep, it's like a pond, or music, you want to sink into. He lists what you must depend on: affection, reading, knowledge, inspiration, and finally patience, "for patience joins time / to eternity."

Have patience with everything that remains unsolved in your heart. Try to love the questions themselves, *like locked rooms and like books written in a foreign language.*

— RAINER MARIA RILKE

85. Motivation

Stanislavski's book *An Actor Prepares* was my bible when I was an actress. Reading my underlined copy now, I realize how pertinent all this Russian wisdom about acting can be for writers. "Don't act 'in general,' for the sake of action; always act with a purpose," writes Stanislavski. "If an action has no inner foundation, it cannot hold your attention."

What is my motivation? is a question method actors ask themselves before doing a scene. *What do I want and need?* This is vital for writers too, in both fiction and nonfiction. Think about what's at stake in every scene you write, what your characters — or you, if it's nonfiction — are after. This need, this want, becomes the subtext of every compelling scene, acted or written.

The writer, like the murderer, needs a motive.

— JANET MALCOLM

86. Looking vs. Seeing

"To begin with," writes Stanislavski, "take a little flower, or a petal from it, or a spider web.... Try to express in words what it is in these that gives pleasure." Trying to get students to pay attention, he says, "An actor should be observant not only on stage, but also in real life."

Writers too.

There's a difference, of course, between looking and seeing. To truly *see* something you need to quiet the chatter in your head. You need to get out of your own way.

Pay attention.... Pay attention. That is all you have to do. Never, for an instant, leave off paying attention.

— THORNTON WILDER

87. Lessons of Drama

Once I was doing a scene in acting class, and I was *really*, *really* acting — sad, scared, distraught, choked with tears! I now forget what the scene was from; but in it someone had left or died, and I was *bereft*. At the end of the scene my acting teacher didn't say anything. There was a long silence.

Finally he told us about an actress in an old film he had seen years before. A war was going on, and the actress was playing a mother who had lost one of her sons. She stood under a tree, watching her second son go off to war — and she kept herself from crying, from showing emotion, but you could see the effort, the courage, without her moving a muscle or making a sound.

I think about this every time I want to stuff the page with dramatic adjectives or ringing adverbs and *really, really* write.

There's nothing that sooner reveals a writer's skill, or lack of it, than his use of the adjective.
— JOHN FAIRFAX and JOHN MOAT, *The Way to Write*

88. From the Desk of God

Writing a novel is like living in a parallel universe. A universe that, unlike reality, you can more or less control. Every day, you find your characters sitting around like polite house-guests waiting to see what you have planned for them. It can be exhilarating on good days, and on other days so difficult and frustrating you think your head might explode. But if you keep showing up, they usually keep showing up too, and eventually you can get them into action.

As a teenager, one of my daughters informed me that she was not one of my characters and I couldn't boss her around. For my birthday that year she gave me notepads that had printed at the top in large letters underlined with a lightning bolt: "FROM THE DESK OF GOD."

The writer becomes the god of his little universe and is amazed by what seems to be spontaneous creation, but is in fact the reward for hard work.

— ROBERT MCKEE

89. Worries of Writing Memoir

Robin Romm worried whether to publish the memoir she had written about the last three weeks of her mother's life. She wrote thirty pages of notes during those weeks, then ninety pages in the ten days after her mother died. Romm felt there were more reasons not to write a memoir than to write it, and asked herself the questions many of us struggle with: "Will people think I am using a tragedy for personal gain? Would my mother like being portrayed sick in a book? Is it a trespass to tell other people's stories? What right did I have to them? Will I be disowned? Will critics be mean? Will some petty blogger go, 'Egads, another cancer book!' I could fill a page with these questions."

But then she read her mother's journals and came across an entry in which her mother, who was an attorney, wrote that she felt her sphere of influence had been so small in this world. "And I had a moment of thinking," says Romm, "that maybe her story, my story, our story, would find its way into the hands of others in the middle of a tragedy, or those trying to help someone in tragedy's clutches. That this story — so small, really, just a mother's death — might have the power to be more universal."

I felt what I felt and I knew what I felt and I wrote what I felt.
— ROBIN ROMM

90. The Wrestling Match

If that pessimistic bird on your shoulder squawking about your lack of talent, that carping voice in your head, that pounding of doom in your chest, is battling with the confidence and drive that got you to sit down to write in the first place, know what good company you're in. I believe writers who never go through this battle are perhaps a wee bit smug. As Brenda Ueland wrote, the glib writers see the ocean as only knee-deep. "If you are never satisfied with what you write," she said, "that is a good sign."

Every single piece of writing I have ever completed — whether a novel, a memoir, an essay, short story or review — has begun as a wrestling match between hopelessness and something else, some other quality that all writers, if they are to keep going, must possess.

— DANI SHAPIRO

91. Naming Names

When I wrote a memoir, I referred to my husband as "R.," which is what I call him in my journal. It felt more natural to call him this in my book, but my editor in New York thought it sounded a bit coy. So I left it up to my husband, and when I asked him what name he wanted in the memoir, Robert or Bob or R., he said he wanted to be called Tom. But he was cheerful about it, and I did not rename him Tom; I stuck with R. If you're writing fiction, this name business isn't much of a problem; you can go to the phone book, come up with a list of names, and then try them on your characters like costumes. Anne Lamott says you can solve the problem of guys announcing they're a character in your novel by describing that character as having a very small penis.

But for real people in nonfiction, things are more complicated. For one thing, lawyers can require that family and friends mentioned in a memoir legally promise they won't sue. I heard one memoir writer tell how she wrote a hymn of praise to the sexual prowess of an ex-husband so he'd sign off for the lawyers. And he did.

I've always thought my creative life began the moment my mother named me Twyla....She had big plans for me. She wanted me to be singular, so she gave me a singular name.

— Twyla Tharp

92. Rituals of Discipline

When John Grisham started writing, he had rituals that he called "silly and brutal but very important." His goal was to write one page a day. His alarm would go off at 5:00, he'd take a shower, and then he'd sit down with coffee and a legal pad by 5:30 to write. He'd do this five days a week. Sometimes he'd write his one page in ten minutes; sometimes it would take two hours. Then he'd go to his day job as a lawyer. "So I was very disciplined about it," he said.

The wonderful thing about discipline is that, unlike inspiration and talent, it's always available to everyone.

Even talent is rarely distinguishable, over the long run, from perseverance and lots of hard work.
— DAVID BAYLES and TED ORLAND, *Art & Fear*

93. Habits of Writers

I know it can take some of the drama and zing out of things, but frankly, writing needs to become a habit. A habit takes the decision out of whether you're going to do something or not; it simply becomes part of your life.

A writing life is built by habit, page by page, with a few perks thrown in — like indulging in buying books or making many visits to the library because your reading is another habit. Or not feeling guilty for going on a binge at Staples or Office Depot.

Maybe you start carrying around a paperback or your ebook that you read every time you're standing in line or waiting in a doctor's office. Or you become obsessive about having a pen and notebook next to every single chair in your house. Or you start taking long walks every morning to think about what you're going to write that day.

I read somewhere that it takes three weeks to make or break a habit. It doesn't have to be a big deal — just begin.

Writers are people who desperately need habits to fill up their days.
— ANN PATCHETT

94. Lighting Candles

Maybe the word *ritual* is a more exciting take on the idea of habit. Brushing your teeth might spring to mind when I say *habit*, but *ritual* is more like Julia Alvarez lighting candles in her writing room, or Anne Rivers Siddons putting her house in order before she begins work on a new book, or Gail Godwin lighting incense. Stephen King has to have a glass of water or a cup of tea when he sits down to write — between 8:00 and 8:30 — and the same seat, the papers arranged the same way. Stravinsky played a Bach fugue every morning when he went to his studio to work.

I had a ritual once of lighting a candle and writing by its light and blowing it out when I was done for the night....Also kneeling and praying before starting (I got that from a French movie about George Frederick Handel).

— JACK KEROUAC

95. Five Things Writers Can Learn from Dogs

1. Be tenacious and curious about everything.
2. Abandon yourself to joy on occasion.
3. At all times, follow what you love.
4. Have a steadfast and loyal heart.
5. Work hard and sleep well.

I could claim any number of high-flown reasons for writing, just as you can explain certain dog behavior as submission to the alpha or even a moral choice. But maybe it's that they're dogs and that's what dogs do.

— AMY HEMPEL

96. The Things We Keep

A photo of Jonathan Franzen's office chair, which appeared to be held together by duct tape, was featured in an *LA Times* article about what writers keep in their offices. Ian Rankin had a photograph of a sign that read "The Oxford Bar," a place he believed a character he writes about would feel at home, and Will Self had hundreds of Post-its of observations, dialogue, themes, etc., stuck to a wall. On her desk A. S. Byatt kept a creature with big yellow eyes and a tail, whose head came off to make an inkwell.

Madeleine L'Engle kept a small white laughing Buddha sitting on her desk that she said prevented her from taking herself too seriously. She believed that he was telling her: "What matters is the book itself. If it is as good a book as you can write at this moment in time, that is what counts."

Another lesson in getting out of your own way.

My white china Buddha is an icon. . . . He laughs at me, never with ridicule, but lovingly.

— MADELEINE L'ENGLE

97. Clear Language

"Clarity, clarity, clarity," said E. B. White.

Grace, at age four, understands this. She has her mother dial my number, and when I answer, she says, "Your horse is dead?" My horse in Montana is indeed dead, and everyone else in the family carefully avoids the subject. "Is it true you put him to death?" she asks. I want to explain that I had to have him *put down*, or *put to sleep* — but Grace has no patience with euphemisms. "Yes," I say.

"That's very sad," she says.

When my cat Charlotte dies a year later, Grace calls soon afterward and says, "Charlotte is dead?" When I say yes, there's a pause and then she asks, "What did you do with her body?"

No one else has asked me this, and I love Grace's directness in finding out the facts, and her impatience with euphemisms that veil those facts. I love her clarity.

Tell one story truly and with clarity and you have done all that anyone is required to do.

— ELLEN GILCHRIST

98. Ideas in Limos and Planes

You just never know where and when ideas can come. Here's how Paul McCartney and John Lennon wrote "Eight Days a Week": McCartney was in a limo on his way to see Lennon, and he asked the chauffeur how he'd been. The chauffeur replied, "Working hard, working eight days a week." When McCartney mentioned this to Lennon, they sat down and wrote the song.

Billy Mernit once played piano and sang backup for Carly Simon, and on a flight to New York with her one day, he noticed reflections in her coffee cup. "Clouds in your coffee," he said.

You can't just dance or paint or write or sculpt. Those are just verbs. You need a tangible idea to get you going. The idea, however minuscule, is what turns the verb into a noun.

— TWYLA THARP

99. Writing Your Own Corner

The world — or the part we humans are in charge of — is a mess. A huge, unconquerable mess. You cannot fix it, nor can you put it all on the page to create a vast novel that encompasses and somehow solves the chaos. All you can do is write your own small corner of this world, how you, or the characters you make up, see it, feel it, and are affected by it. And maybe figure out one tiny thing in the chaos that you can help make right or illuminate.

To me, now, to do something new is not to develop a form for the novel that has never been seen on earth before. It means to try to come to terms as a person and a citizen with what's happening in the world now and to do it in some comprehensible, coherent way.

— JONATHAN FRANZEN

100. Writing as Therapy

Maybe you couldn't care less about becoming a writer. Maybe you don't want to get published. Maybe you simply want to write down your feelings and thoughts because you feel better when you do; you get the snarl, the sadness, the I-will-kill-that-person out of your system. Maybe writing feels dangerous to you because someone might find what you write. Which is really just another version of standing in your own way. You can burn what you write! Yes, watch it go up in flames, or you can write it in code, or hide it really, really well.

And it's a whole lot cheaper than psychotherapy.

But you know the real reason it feels dangerous? Because once you start writing, who knows what you'll find out about yourself.

I think I have no real escape except through this. These few fragile words I can manage every day. I must think, I must let myself explore what I am feeling and thinking. I need to explore that black territory.

— SANDY DENNIS

101. Waiting for the Train

David Vann began a novel and had to put it aside because of technical difficulties he couldn't solve. But when he returned to it fourteen years later, the writing came very quickly, like a "freight train."

"That's not what's supposed to happen," he said in an interview. "I guess my writing process is screwy. I kept returning to the landscape and to the characters, and that just allowed the story to take off."

I would love to hear about a writing process that isn't screwy.

I wrote in tiny tiny writing on tiny tiny Post-its, which I would stick to the wall and collect in the morning.

— ALICE W. FLAHERTY

102. Five Things Writers Can Learn from Cats

1. Stay focused.
2. Retain mystery.
3. Hunt (i.e., take notes) quietly.
4. Be independent.
5. Be still and silent for long periods of time.

As for writers and cats, there's something very internal about cats. Cats like to go out, but they do so in a stealthy manner. Writers, even though they might be sociable and extroverted, have to draw on their subterranean, internal qualities, and since the cat embodies these qualities, it may help the writer invoke them.

— MARY GAITSKILL

103. Closing the Gap

When it comes to reading, I have good taste. I'm in love with writing that's graceful, smart, wise, articulate, and honest. I'm in awe of writers who can put life on the page and make our world wider and deeper.

Ira Glass says that we get into creative work because of our good taste. But then there's a gap between our own art and what we admire. In the beginning our work only has potential. We're disappointed because it just doesn't measure up to our good taste, and the only way to close the gap is by doing a lot of work. He says it took him longer to figure this out than anyone he knows, but I'm not sure about that. I have to figure it out every time I sit down to write.

And if you are just starting out or you are still in this phase, you gotta know it's normal and the most important thing you can do is do a lot of work. Put yourself on a deadline so that every week you will finish one story.

— Ira Glass

104. Writing Your Own Front Yard

During the two years Ted Kooser was poet laureate of the United States, traveling a lot and giving talks and interviews, he wrote in his journal daily, but very few poems came; he said he didn't have time for the contemplative life necessary for poetry. The first poem he wrote during this period was about his dog and its bone. "What matters," he said, "is what happens in your own front yard."

I am a writer who came of a sheltered life. A sheltered life can be a daring life as well. For all serious daring starts from within.

— EUDORA WELTY

105. PERFECTION!

There's a very scary board game called Perfection. It's one of my worst nightmares. You set a timer and have sixty seconds to put dozens of small yellow plastic pieces of various shapes into dozens of matching holes. The timer ticking sounds like the opening of *60 Minutes* on steroids. Axel, at age seven, loves this game, and he's very good at it. I am not good at it. "Hey, BABS, it's FUN!" he yells. (He speaks in capitals when he's excited.)

"This is not my idea of fun," I say. BECAUSE when the timer goes off, there's this TERRIFYING snap, and all the pieces explode up into the air. This seems a lot like writing to me. The clock is always ticking, the pieces don't fit, the whole thing feels like it's going to explode, and all we want is PERFECTION.

Perfectionism is the voice of the oppressor, the enemy of the people. It will keep you cramped and insane your whole life, and it is the main obstacle between you and a shitty first draft.

— ANNE LAMOTT

106. Odd Notes

Every time I attempt to organize my office, strange notes rise up. Most are not only incomplete but also incomprehensible: "My mother is saving the wings of termites to..." To *what*? *Whose* mother? What was I thinking when I wrote that? If I should die in a sudden accident, my family would be mystified and probably disturbed to read these odd notes and exhortations. "Take a left turn in your own material" or "What is safe? What does *safe* mean?" (those two notes for this book, I think). And then: "Does M. ever sleep with N.? If she does, she has to tell H." (this from a novel that has yet to get off the ground). A writer's notes can sound like the musings of a person who's not terribly well.

However, every book I've ever written has started with an odd note.

I might as well make a note I say to myself: thinking sometimes who's going to read all this scribble? I think one day I may brew a tiny ingot out of it — in my memoirs.

— Virginia Woolf

107. A Love Story

From 1920 to 1924, Robinson Jeffers built a stone tower with his own hands for his beloved wife, Una, who adored the stone towers of Ireland. The tower Jeffers built was next to their cottage, Tor House, in Carmel, California, and he hauled the stones himself up from the beach every afternoon after he worked on his poems in the morning. The granite stones, boulders really, some weighing over three hundred pounds, are a perfect metaphor for writing, and being a stonemason is perhaps the perfect day job for a poet.

When answering a questionnaire that asked, "What distinguishes you from the ordinary man?" Jeffers wrote, "Nothing essential; a little specialization."

It's the ideal situation for me. I like the physical endeavors that go with the farm — cutting hay, cleaning out stalls, or building a barn. You go do that and then come back to the writing.

— SAM SHEPARD

108. Aunt Boo's House

The Jefferses' cottage in Carmel, Tor House, remains today, half a century after Robinson Jeffers's death, with the dishes and photographs, inkwells and piano, books and furniture, and hundreds of precious objects intact. Including the bed where Jeffers died. The docent who gives tours knows all the stories because Una Jeffers kept a meticulous inventory of what they owned and the history of everything.

I spent a summer in Carmel when I was eight years old, staying with my aunt. Years later, after touring Tor House, I found what I thought was my aunt's house on Santa Fe Road. I *think* it was Aunt Boo's house — old Spanish, two blocks up from the village, and a chimney that looked like it could have been the one I remembered in the living room — but everyone who would have known whether in fact this was her house is now gone. And with them, the memory of all the things that house held, the stories and history, has vanished. Nothing was written down.

Writers are the custodians of memory, and memories have a way of dying with their owner.

— WILLIAM ZINSSER

109. Just Reading

Remember when you were a kid and some adult would say, "Put that book down and go outside"? Or "Stop reading and do your homework!"? Well, now you're not only an adult but also a writer, so no one can ever again tell you to put the book down. Besides, when you're sitting there "just" reading, you *are* at work.

Like most, maybe all writers, I learned to write by writing and, by example, from books.

— FRANCINE PROSE

110. Reading in Russia

Sometimes I have to think twice if I actually know authors as friends in real life or just feel that I know them because I've read and connected to their books. Some books deepen your life, put into words what you feel but never have articulated before, and you find yourself nodding, yes, yes, as you read, that's the way it is, and you feel as if you've found a true friend.

Once on a trip to Russia I read a book that I fell so much in love with that I had to email the author immediately. "I'm in Moscow reading *The Journal Keeper*!" I wrote to Phyllis Theroux — who I found on Facebook. I told her I had her memoir on my ebook reader but loved it so much I had just ordered a hard copy, and thanked her for such a deep and delicious read. The next day I heard back from her. What a miracle, I thought, what an amazing thing to be reading a book in Russia and start an email conversation with a writer you admire and have become friends with.

Behold, nothing surpasses books. Would that I might make you love them more than your mother. Would that I might make their beauty enter before your face. For it is greater than any office. You are to set your heart on books.

— ANONYMOUS, 2150 BCE

111. Authors on Pedestals

One my favorite authors, Mark Salzman, gave a performance piece at the Los Angeles Public Library about his decade-long case of writer's block. He said that when his girls were born and he took on the role of the stay-at-home parent, he told himself, "I'll write during the kids' naps! Fatherhood will inspire me." Fatherhood certainly did inspire him, but not to write. He was exhausted, and when his babies napped, so did he. Creating the performance piece was what helped him to break through his writer's block and to eventually write a memoir, *The Man in the Empty Boat*. "Not thinking I was writing something to be read freed me up a lot," he said.

After his monologue, when he signed copies of his book, I mentioned that my daughters lived in the same town as he did and told him their last names. He said, "Axel! He lives down the street from us." Later, when I told my daughters about this, they were surprised Salzman was so well known, and said they often saw him picking up his girls from school.

Even as they churn out their elegant prose and get on the *New York Times* bestseller list, our favorite authors get stuck and blocked in their work, diaper the babies, pick up the kids at school, and sometimes, amazingly, live right down the street from our family.

Writing is an ideal occupation if you're a rabbit. It gives you an excuse to stay in your burrow all day, and it allows you to explore problems like anguish and insecurity without having to solve them. You don't need to have peace of mind to be a writer; in fact, the more troubled you feel, the more you have to write about.

— Mark Salzman

112. Getting to Denver by 4:00

Though writers can do magic, transformations, etc., we are not so special that we can't sit down to do our work if we're not in the mood. Think of a surgeon not in the mood to do a heart bypass at 7:00 AM, or the truck driver too uninspired to get the truck to Denver by 4:00, or the rancher who doesn't feel like hauling out the hay for the cows some icy December morning. We sit down and start writing, in the mood or not.

Deciding to procrastinate is deciding not to write.

— Ted Kooser and Steve Cox,
Writing Brave & Free

113. Surrender

Surrender to your own ego. Let yourself sound dumb, dull, or overly earnest, or whatever you fear most about your own writing. Surrender and then rewrite.

Poetry demands surrender, language saying what is true, doing holy things to the ordinary.

— Pamela Spiro Wagner

114. The Idea That Won't Go Away

It's the idea that won't go away that you must write about. When Kim Edwards heard a story in church that would become the basic plot of *The Memory Keeper's Daughter*, she thought it would make a really good novel, but she didn't believe it was her story to write.

But years went by, and she couldn't get the idea out of her head. Things happened in her life that made her believe that perhaps the idea was hers to write about after all.

So far the book has sold 4.1 million copies.

I tell you this not to raise your hopes for fortune and fame but to show how easily a good idea that touched millions of people could have slipped away.

Every story has a story.

— Patricia Hampl

115. Writing the Tree

When beginning one of his first stories, William Saroyan asked himself why he was writing about "the old English walnut tree in the backyard of the rickety frame house at 2226 San Benito Avenue in Fresno."

Writing that tree (whose hard fruit he used as a perfect metaphor for how we write and how we read) finally led him to the parlor piano, where there was a picture of his kid brother who was killed in the war.

There is no how to it, no how do you write, no how do you live, how do you die.... It is the doing that makes for continuance. It is not the knowing of how the doing is done.

— WILLIAM SAROYAN

116. Why Writers Get Scared

Hoping to impress her, I showed Emma, age nine, a YouTube video of me reading an essay at a publication event. At first she was impressed that I was even on YouTube. But then, as she listened to the essay I was reading, she suddenly yelled, "Babs, you're telling all your secrets!"

"Well, that's what writers do," I said.

She was now horrified, not impressed. "I would *never* do that," she said.

Most people don't and won't. That's why it's scary for writers. You can shock nine-year-old kids.

And because I found I had nothing else to write about, I presented myself as a subject.

— Michel de Montaigne

117. The Loneliness of the Long-Distance Writer

Writing can be a lonely business. But gradually your characters, or the scenes and people from your past, begin to rise up around you, and you find yourself writing your way out of loneliness, writing your own company. And you'll find yourself at dinner some evening telling your family or friends, "Well, Natalie really made a mess of things today" or "I can't believe what John said about Kathryn's dog." And everyone will look at you mystified because Natalie and John and Kathryn — and the dog — reside only in your head; you've made them up.

I am learning to see loneliness as a seed that, when planted deep enough, can grow into writing that goes back out into the world.

— KATHLEEN NORRIS

118. Infusion of Hope: The Circus Rider

When Julia Alvarez was thirty-four years old, she was a struggling writer, divorced with no children, and felt like a failure. One day she found courage in a museum she had passed every day on the way to work but had never gone into, the Phillips Collection in Washington, DC. When she finally went in, she fell in love with a painting — Pierre Bonnard's *The Circus Rider*. Years later Alvarez said she identified with the little circus rider on top of a powerful horse, holding on with purpose, while the circus-goers in the background, all dressed in black, looking like judges, waited for the rider to falter.

"She just stayed focused," said Alvarez. "She didn't look down, because she would get terrified … and fall off. She didn't look up at the figures of judgment because she would've gotten scared that they were being critical of her. She just stayed focused. And I thought, she's telling me how to do this. So all that year, when I would have to give a big reading or teach a workshop, I would drop in and get my little infusion of hope. I really think she carried me through that year."

There's a great lesson in it — it's all about the work. It's not about what people might say or about how dangerous it might get. But it's about staying focused on what you do, and doing what you love.
— JULIA ALVAREZ

119. Stillness

To be engaged in reading a book or in writing, to connect to your inner life, goes against everything contemporary life, with all its bells and whistles, is about. To be quiet, to be still, in this loud, raucous world can be scary. But sometimes just acknowledging that fact helps to take some of the fear away.

The place of stillness that you have to go to write, but also to read seriously, is the point where you can actually make responsible decisions, where you can actually engage productively with an otherwise scary and unmanageable world.

— JONATHAN FRANZEN

120. Writing the Event

Thoreau said that there are two kinds of writing: one reports the event; the other is the event itself. This is another version of show-don't-tell. One is at arm's length; the other is right in your face, in your heart, in your senses. When you read the event itself, you forget that you're reading — you're experiencing it. And we write and we rewrite to discover how to do this with every story.

And the great moment in writing something is when you realize that the wonderful, unheard-of event you just made up is part of the wonderful, heard-of event of life itself.

— ROGER ROSENBLATT

121. Life Rafts

Certain books on my shelves act as life rafts when I'm drowning in my own writing. During one particular novel I'd been struggling with for years that had been rejected, I reread a chapter in Anne Lamott's *Bird by Bird*. In it she writes about the completed manuscript of one of her novels being rejected *after* it was sold and she'd spent most of the advance for it. She pulled herself together, spread the three hundred pages of her manuscript across the living room floor, rearranged and reimagined the scenes, and then rewrote it. It went well; she was euphoric. She borrowed money, flew to New York to see her editor, who had just read it, and he said to her, "I'm so, so sorry, but it still doesn't work." Then, after all her disappointment and humiliation and anger and ranting, she went off and wrote five hundred to a thousand words every day describing what was happening in each chapter and who her characters really were. She came up with a forty-page plot treatment of the book, showed it to her editor, and rewrote the book again. It was published the following fall.

I figured out, over and over, point A, where the chapter began, and point B, where it ended, and what needed to happen to get my people from A to B. And then how the B of the last chapter would lead organically into point A of the next chapter. The book moved along like the alphabet, like a vivid and continuous dream.

— ANNE LAMOTT

122. Fiction vs. Nonfiction

"Writing fiction is for me a fraught business, an occasion of daily dread for at least the first half of the novel, and sometimes all the way through," says Joan Didion. "The work process is totally different from writing nonfiction. You have to sit down every day and make it up."

Robin Romm says, "Fiction is more difficult, I think, than memoir. Not only do you need to depict the world in all its detail, and characters in all their complexity, you also need to figure out what's going to happen. In memoir, you know what's going to happen."

But then Lee Smith says, "Writing an essay is like pulling teeth, compared to writing fiction."

Gay Talese thinks nonfiction writers are second-class citizens, "the Ellis Island of Literature." "We just can't quite get in," he says. "And yes, it pisses me off."

When you write nonfiction you have to at least pretend to be a person of some unflappable normalcy who is making reasonable judgments. Fiction, on the other hand, allows you to be a little more provisional and vulnerable, and truer.

— NICHOLSON BAKER

123. An Empty Swimming Pool

Sebastian Junger started out working as a high climber for tree-removal companies, and after a chain saw injury he switched to journalism. Now he writes nonfiction books about people with dangerous jobs — the military, firefighters, and fishermen (which led to *The Perfect Storm*). The only thing he appears to be frightened of is writing fiction. He says, "Writing fiction feels like it would be like going off a diving board into a swimming pool that has no water in it."

And this is exactly what novelists do, isn't it? Create the water and fill the pool.

A bad novel is hard to write. A brilliant novel, like I don't even know how that happens.

— SEBASTIAN JUNGER

124. Breaking Glass:
Metaphor and Symbols

In the past two years I've had windows break in my house, my car, and my cabin. What does this mean? One was a weird fluke of wind that blew out a French door that then smacked into an outside light, shattering panes of glass. Another was caused when I clicked my garage opener at the wrong moment and the rear window of my car splintered; and the third was vandalism, a rock into my cabin window. I've cleaned up all this broken glass and discussed it with insurance companies, though I'm not sure where the metaphor of broken glass can go. But if I keep coming back to it, keep it in my head, it will eventually connect with something else. Metaphor is about connections, and that's what writing is all about too — connecting the dots. Figuring it out, finding patterns, even in shards of glass. Or maybe all this glass is simply a symbol of fragility; nothing is safe. Or maybe it's actually about windows.

Or maybe, like Gertrude Stein's rose, broken glass is broken glass is broken glass.

I never try to make metaphors. My flag is staked on the turf of the literal. Metaphors are things people make out of the literal stuff of life. They are abstractions. They are expressions of language which unite two otherwise disparate things.

— RICHARD FORD

125. Approval

In 1953 Ray Bradbury wrote an article published in the *Nation* defending his work as a science-fiction writer, and a few weeks later he received a letter from Bernard Berenson stating, "In 89 years of life, this is the first fan letter I have written." Bradbury couldn't believe the great art historian had written to him (with an invitation, no less, to visit him in Florence if he ever came to Italy). Bradbury was thirty-three years old and needed that approval. We all need approval and acceptance, and perhaps as writers, working alone without paychecks or coworkers, we need it more than most people.

We all need someone higher, wiser, older to tell us we're not crazy after all, that what we're doing is all right.

— RAY BRADBURY

126. The Art of Finding Solitude

Naomi Shihab Nye writes about the preciousness of time in her poem "The Art of Disappearing." She tells you what you should think before you reply to a party invitation or when people want to use up your time, why and how to preserve solitude. And she tells you the important things you must try to remember: "Trees. The monastery bell at twilight."

Solitude fills up the well.

"Art is the apotheosis of solitude," said Samuel Beckett.

Marge Piercy keeps Monday evenings for herself. Alone from 7:00 until 10:00, she turns off the phone and computer, thinks "long and hard" about her life, and then does deep meditation that she says "feels holy and healing." "This practice," she says, "is part of how I stay sane and productive and open to others."

Creative work needs solitude. It needs concentration, without interruptions. It needs the whole sky to fly in, and no eye watching until it comes to that certainty which it aspires to, but does not necessarily have at once. Privacy, then. A place apart.

— MARY OLIVER

127. One True Sentence

In *A Moveable Feast* Ernest Hemingway writes, "I would stand and look out over the roofs of Paris and think, 'Do not worry. You have always written before and you will write now. All you have to do is write one true sentence. Write the truest sentence that you know.' So finally I would write one true sentence, and then go from there. It was easy then because there was always one true sentence that I knew or had seen or had heard someone say."

Hemingway believed that if he started to write in a fancy way, he could go back and then start with the first simple declarative sentence he'd written.

It's odd reading Hemingway now; his simple declarative sentences sound like he's imitating Hemingway, as if in spite of himself he got trapped in a lie of style. But the advice to himself to write just one true sentence still works.

For what is writing, after all, but a bid for the truth? And what is truth if not the life at the very heart of failure?

— LYNN FREED

128. Learning to Swim

I learned to swim from a magazine article I read when I was eight years old. It told me to grab my knees, duck my head, form a tight little ball in the water, and then float. The next step was to stretch out and continue to float. I did exactly what the article said to do, and lo and behold, it worked. I got my arms going at some point, and I was a swimmer.

It's kind of like writing: get a paper and a pen, start with a writing prompt — and you're writing. Faith that you'll float and not sink has a lot to do with it.

I think that is...the secret of writing: attitude. Hope, unyielding faith in the enterprise.

— BARBARA KINGSOLVER

129. Imaginations Going Nuts

As writers, we have such vivid imaginations that we're also able to imagine, in flaming detail, possible failures ahead — rejections of biblical proportions, a bag lady future, being sued by our dearest and closest relatives, as well as mulling over the possibility of airline/car/train crashes, incurable viruses, natural disasters, etc.

It's just your imagination not having enough to do — put it back to work in your story.

I don't know why my imagination takes me where it does. I just feel so lucky to get a single idea for a novel that I can write about.
— JOSEPH HELLER

130. Paying Attention

Why write? Because you're alive and breathing and the natural world is a miraculous place that needs to be loved and celebrated and remembered. You do this by paying attention and writing down what you see and hear and smell and touch and taste.

Sometimes it's that simple.

Why should we have been born knowing how to love the world? We require again and again these demonstrations.

— MARK DOTY

131. Do Not Try This at Home

Susan Sontag didn't write regularly because she had so many other things she loved to do — travel, go out every night, see friends. But when she did write, she'd clear big chunks of time and work around the clock, usually fueled by Dexedrine. Sigrid Nunez, who lived with Sontag's son, David Rieff, said they'd go to sleep to the sound of her typing and the next morning wake up to it. Sontag wished she could work in a less self-destructive way, but "she believed it was only after going at it full throttle for many hours that your mind really started to click and you'd come up with your best ideas."

My first feeling about everything I write is that it's shit.
— SUSAN SONTAG

132. Double-Edged Sword of the Internet

The Internet, of course, is a blessing for writers — all that information to be had literally at your fingertips, and if you're publishing a book, your agent and your editor are seconds away via email. On the other hand, it's a curse — everybody else you know, and don't know, is seconds away on email too, or on Facebook or wherever your electronic village resides on your computer. Plus the double-edged sword of all that information at your fingertips.

Jonathan Franzen writes on an old Dell laptop disconnected from the Internet — the wireless card removed and the Ethernet port permanently blocked. "What you have to do," he says, "is you plug in an Ethernet cable with superglue, and then you saw off the little head of it."

The reformed e-mail addict may now find that chatting at the cybercafé is more and more eating into his writing time. If the force driving him first to e-mail and then to the café is the loneliness of writing, a simple change such as working at the café, among the comfortable buzz of other customers, might be enough.

— ALICE W. FLAHERTY

133. Hearing Voices

In spite of Franzen's tricks to disconnect from the Internet, the novel he was working on, *Freedom*, didn't go well. He hated what he wrote and he got stuck. By 2008, after seven years of work, he had accomplished just one thing for the novel: a voice. "This discontented suburban mom who had a certain kind of laugh, and a certain kind of sarcasm, and a certain kind of rage," he said.

Finding your own voice on the page, or the voice for your characters, can fly into your head like a sudden miracle, or it can take, well, seven years.

You must find the right voice (or voices)...that can convince a reader to give himself up to you. Sometimes it takes years to find the tone of voice that unlocks the story.

— ERICA JONG

134. The Key

The key to becoming a writer is a paradox: You must believe that your writing, your story, is important, vital, and a sacred task. At the same time you must be able to write even when you believe absolutely none of the above is true and when writing feels like a job that you're not very good at.

This is not unlike a marriage or rearing children.

Lower your standards and keep writing.
— WILLIAM STAFFORD

135. Mentors

We all need a mentor — someone who will have faith in us and, most of all, inspire us, give us a working model of how to be a writer. Michael Korda, thanks to family connections, was able to observe Graham Greene at work — rising at dawn and writing exactly five hundred words (no matter if he had to stop midparagraph) and then going out into the world to lead a glamorous life for the rest of the day. This seemed pretty impressive to a teenage Korda, who grew up to become Greene's publisher.

Greene's manuscripts would arrive on Korda's desk with this note: "Please do not change any of Mr. Greene's punctuation or spelling!"

Why do I write? Because the person I wanted to be came down and sat with us from time to time and showed us what he was working on, as if to say that what we were doing was all the same thing.... Mentors are extremely hard to come by.

— Ann Patchett

136. Another View of Mentors

I found my mentor at a community college when I took my first writing course. I came in with a really bad novel that I had spent six years on and was scared to death, and quite possibly if my teacher, Norma Almquist, hadn't been the gentle, smart, inspiring soul she was, I may never have found the courage to keep writing.

On the other hand, the opposite approach obviously worked for Francine du Plessix Gray, whose poetry teacher, Charles Olson, yelled at her, "Girl, this is pure shit! You're going to do nothing but keep a journal for a year, an hour a day at a minimum!" She did exactly this, and when she showed Olson her journal a year later, he started yelling again, calling it conservative junk. He told her not to try to publish anything for *ten years*. Again she followed his advice, and exactly one year past that deadline she published her first story in the *New Yorker*.

Getting your pages back from [Annie Dillard] was like getting to the dance floor and seeing your favorite black shirt under the nightclub's blacklight, all the hair and dust that was always there but invisible to you now visible.

— ALEXANDER CHEE

137. Mileage from Childhood Fears

Maurice Sendak intended for *Where the Wild Things Are* to be *Where the Wild Horses Are*; but he couldn't draw horses, so he switched to wild things. The monsters he drew were caricatures of his relatives who visited every Sunday when he was a little boy growing up in Brooklyn. As his mother cooked dinner, he was afraid his aunts and uncles would say to him, "You look so good, we could eat you up!" — and since food was scarce in those days, he feared the literal truth of those words.

He was also terrified of vacuum cleaners as a child, so when *Where the Wild Things Are* (only 385 words long) was made into an opera and needed more scenes, he wrote an opening in which Max's mother enters with an old Hoover vacuum that drives Max to attack it with his sword.

Sendak once said that the things that scared him as a child probably frightened him into being an artist.

People think I have some magic link to my childhood. If there is such a link, it's a process that bypasses my conscious mind, because I have very little real recollection. I couldn't stop and tell you why I'm writing and drawing certain episodes; they're coming from some inner source that does recollect.

— MAURICE SENDAK

138. Writer Panic Attacks

The occasional panic attack is perfectly fine; it can provide you with needed adrenaline and regrouping. When I panic, I go first to my journal and then to my calculator. In my journal I become extremely self-pitying and allow the crazed demons of future failure out onto the page. Then I write some goals.

With my calculator I figure out how many pages I need and how many days to reach my goals. This happens over and over; I go from drama queen to accountant.

Oh that my words were now written! Oh that they were printed in a book!

— JOB 19:23

139. Your Road

Let's call your writing a journey that you're taking. Only you know what road to take, how fast you should go, and where you're headed. And maybe writing is simply part of the road you're on, one component of your journey. Perhaps you fervently believe in raising chickens in your own backyard, or that the way to happiness is 108 sun salutations every day; so then you're writing a book about this, and basically your road is all about chickens or yoga. Or maybe your whole journey, this road ahead, is devoted to writing the great American novel, or coming up with essays to send out every week, or books for kids. Whatever it is, you're passionate about it, and you never take your eyes off the road; you stay on it, and you get where you have to go.

What quickens my pulse now is the stretch ahead rather than the one behind, and it is mainly for some clue to where I am going that I search through where I have been, for some hint as to who I am becoming or failing to become that I delve into what used to be.
— FREDERICK BUECHNER

140. Making Soup

When you get stuck and anxious, when writing becomes a literary endeavor akin to climbing the Himalayas barefoot, think of writing as making soup. You open the fridge and think, *Ah, some carrots here*, and *Those chicken bones might lead to something*, and *What about these old potatoes?* Who knows what will happen if you throw it all in a pot and let it simmer for a while?

You're just fooling around with carrots and chicken bones here. You're trusting that your subconscious is cooking and will simmer its ingredients, that if you keep doing the work — writing down the details, tapping on the keys, or moving pen across paper, remembering and imagining — something delicious will appear.

Stories are what show up on the page once you start hitting the keys.
— LARRY McMURTRY

141. Poetry for Your Table

One of my daughters gave me the gift of words one Christmas, literally. It's a V-shaped wooden stand that holds eight blocks, and each block has a word on each of its six sides. Wonderful words: *wicked*, *screaming*, *trust*, *sex*, *love*. I keep it on the coffee table in the living room, and everyone, including grandchildren, loves to play with it.

But it can make my writer friends a little anxious. One worked with the blocks all through a party, but he wouldn't let me see what he'd put together. He called what he wrote "pretentious, boring lines of poetry."

The kids always treat it like what it is — a game.

I just kept a notebook, starting when I was about twelve, and I wrote down words that I loved the taste of, words such as azalea, *or for some reason* halcyon. . . . *I was a collector of odd words.*

— COLEMAN BARKS

142. Writers with a View

Chimamanda Ngozi Adichie writes that her view in Lagos, Nigeria, is an ordinary view but because it's full of people, the view is "choked with stories": "the stylish young woman who sells phone cards...the Hausa boys who sell water in plastic containers...the bean-hawker who prowls around in the mornings...a large pan on her head."

Perhaps all views looked at long enough become ordinary. But it's the job of writers to not let this happen, to see what's outside our own windows as if we were on a vacation and the view were all brand new.

That said, the view out my own window has become wallpaper. The red tile roof and two white chimneys, the overgrown tree that blocks out most of the beach, the palm trees — I never look at this anymore. But right now, turning away from the wall I face when I'm working on my computer, looking out the window, I notice a man in a yellow jacket biking slowly north, I notice that the surf has turned a pale shade of silver, I see a jogger followed by a large dog: life outside of my own head.

When my writing is not going well, there are two things I do in the hope of luring the words back: I read some pages of books I love or I watch the world.

— CHIMAMANDA NGOZI ADICHIE

143. Marriage vs. Dating

Perhaps you're deep into your book right now, and you're feeling a tiny bit stuck — or massively stuck, as if the top of your head might blow off. Writing a book is like a very long marriage — complete with good times, sex and jokes, and other times when you're arguing about who takes out the garbage, and bills are piling up, and nobody wants to cook. It's easy to get stuck.

Writing a poem or a short essay can be more like dating — no commitment. If things don't work out, you just go on to the next one. Unlike with marriage, it's much easier and simpler to take a break from your book and go off to have a fling with a poem or essay.

Starting a novel isn't so different from starting a marriage. The dreams you pin on these people are enormous.

— ANN PATCHETT

144. Drinking, Bloating, and Not Writing

Sometimes it's helpful to read the journals of famous writers — especially journals not initially written for publication. You'll find that most writers are obsessed with their health, their weight, the weather, and trying to get on with their work. On September 17, 1960, Christopher Isherwood was worried about drinking too much, bloating, his weight (150 pounds), and his new book; and he wrote in his journal, "I have got to stop it and get on with my novel." On March 5, 1962, he wrote: "I still am not getting on with my work. I have to repeat that sentence. Nagging at myself hasn't seemed to help. And yet, it is terribly hard to see just why I don't do more."

In the fall of 1963 he finished the third and final draft of *A Single Man* and wrote: "In case *A Single Man* is later thought to be a masterpiece, may I state that it bores me unutterably to read? Going through it is really a grind." And then, of course, the weather: "The heat is beyond belief. It rises through the floor boards of our balcony." And his health: "My throat is just the same, and I am worried about it, of course."

All this can be helpful — either to take famous writers down from the mountaintop and help us realize they're human beings just like us, or to prove the old saying that misery loves company. A little schadenfreude never hurts.

I sit here trying to write exactly 650 words for Life *about a show of 19th-century American painting, furniture, etc., at the Met.... Over the weekend I almost died of food poisoning.*

— ROBERT PHELPS

145. Talent

Of course, some people have talent. A natural ability to do something — sing, tap-dance, juggle, write. But what I find as a teacher and as an editor is that the writers who succeed are the ones who simply don't give up. I can predict which students are going to get published and take their work the distance, and it's not always the most immediately flashy, talented ones.

Lots of people have talent, darlin'. But look how many people throw it away. It boils down to this: having talent is not enough. You also have to have a talent for having talent.

— RUTH GORDON

146. The Sliver of Ice

Graham Greene famously once said that every writer needed a sliver of ice in his or her heart. Lynn Freed believes that writers need the heart of an assassin. In an interview, Susan Stamberg told Philip Roth about a writer whose mother had sued him, and Roth's response was, "That's a wonderful story! He should write that story!"

This selfishness of the writer to mine his or her own life — joys and tragedies alike — for story, for plot, for theme, is part of being a writer, whether you call it slivers of ice, or turning into an assassin, or being a scavenger. We can't write the truth without it. But that doesn't mean you have to show it to your mother.

I'm basically a treacherous person with no sense of loyalty. I'd write openly about my sainted mother's sex life for art.

— SUSAN BRAUDY

147. Themes

Maybe you know your theme, maybe you don't. You don't need one right now. (I once almost drove a student right out of the classroom with this statement; he was convinced you had to know your theme right off the bat, and I was to teach him how to find it.) The what's-it-all-about, the underlying point of this novel you're writing, the message, the reason for your memoir, poem, short story, the "takeaway" as your agent or editor will call it — well, maybe you just don't have a clue right now what it is. Don't worry about it. Your life has inherent themes and deep values, and one of the reasons we write is to discover what they are.

Beware of general themes. Cling to those that your everyday life offers you.

— RAINER MARIA RILKE

148. Intimacy

I want to read writers who have the courage to let me into their lives, who are open and intimate. If they've gone to the trouble of writing a book or an essay, I want it to be emotionally true; I want the details, the nitty-gritty, what's underneath the facade. This is not to say that I want to read their life *spilled* onto the page but the details, the emotion, their experience crafted into art.

May Sarton wrote, "I believe we learn through the experiences of others as well as through our own, constantly meditating upon them, drawing the substance of human truth from them."

There's no intimacy without truth, and how dangerous it sometimes feels to write it.

We yearn to escape the demons of our subjectivity. We yearn to escape our selves, into intimacy.

— WILLIAM KITTREDGE

149. The DVD in Your Head

Maybe the essay you're writing, or the memoir or novel, has now taken up residence in your inner life, like a DVD playing inside your head. Maybe as you go to sleep at night, you're working on your story, you dream it. And when you brush your teeth in the morning, you're thinking about it, seeing flashbacks of your own life or your characters hovering behind you. If it's a book you're working on, you imagine what the cover will look like. Articles you read in the newspaper or online, things you observe, hear on radio or TV — everything starts to connect to your work.

Maybe you already have a draft of an essay or short story you've written that needs to sit for a while for you to get some perspective on it, and you're looking for the subject of your next one. What you look for you usually find.

Or maybe not. Maybe you're stuck. But the only way to become unstuck is to keep showing up, to keep writing. And trust that when you do show up, something will be playing in your unconscious.

The physical act of sitting at your computer writing down words is important of course but your unconscious mind is also doing a lot of the work for you. If you show up. If you hold your characters in your mind, if you constantly look at the world for ideas to go into your book.

— WALTER MOSLEY

150. Forgetting How to Write

It's like losing the rhythm in a dance or the tune when you're singing. Words turn on you. Sentences become overly complicated, arthritic with anxiety. You suddenly sound like you're teaching something, or worse, that you don't know anything. When this happens to me, there are certain writers I reach for who will remind me what a loose, quirky dance writing can be, and to lighten up a little. When I read Abigail Thomas's memoirs and she blithely goes from first person to third, and into second, and some of her chapters are just a paragraph long — I feel liberated.

The important thing is to look for writers who do this for you, and then to keep their books close at hand. My life raft may not be yours. But yours is out there if you look hard enough.

I remember the waitress calling out, "Adam and Eve on a raft, hold the raft." I remember the booths were cracked red vinyl, none of us ate much of anything, and I think we all smoked Kents, but I don't remember what the raft was.

— ABIGAIL THOMAS

151. Walking Away

Jane Smiley said she felt like she'd wandered into a dark wood when she was two-thirds through a novel she was working on. After winning the Pulitzer Prize and publishing eleven novels in an amazing array of styles and genres, plus three books of nonfiction, she realized she didn't know what she was doing with this novel. She had 125 pages to go. She never finished it.

Instead, she sat down and read one hundred novels, and then wrote and published a 569-page book about what she had read.

I didn't know what in the world I was doing, and it was way too late in the game for that. My heart sank. No, my flesh turned to ice. No, my eyes popped out of my head. No, my stomach churned. No, all I did was close the file on my computer and walk away. But that was very bad.

— JANE SMILEY

152. The Eleven-Day Marathon

Georges Simenon wrote his elegant, short novels in eleven days — a chapter per day. He would live like a monk while he was working; he wouldn't talk, see anyone, or take phone calls. Before the start of each novel, he would see his doctor, who would check him out and tell him whether he was okay for such an intense marathon of writing.

The beginning of each of his novels would always be the same: He had a certain man, a certain woman, in a certain setting. What would push them to go to their limit? He studied maps for his settings and knew those details, but he only knew what would happen in the first chapter when he began to write.

I've found that writing novels is an all-absorbing experience — both physical and mental — and I have to do it every day in order to keep the rhythm, to keep myself focused on what I'm doing. Even Sunday, if possible.... Whenever I travel, I get thrown off completely. If I'm gone for two weeks, it takes me a good week to get back into the rhythm of what I was doing before.

— PAUL AUSTER

153. Writing Your Own Marathon

We do a version of a marathon in class, rounds of five-minute writing prompts, one after another. What happens during a marathon is that people get tired, which is not always a bad thing when you're writing. You let down your guard and stop trying so hard. You can't wait for inspiration — you just do it. When each round is read aloud without comments, the emotions, the scenes from everyone's life, create a communal feel to writing — we're all in this together — and stories blend.

A marathon could also be done with a writing buddy or in a small group of writers or even alone. It's a good way to break through a stuck place in a manuscript. You could collect writing prompts, either writing your own or cutting them from newspapers, and put them in a basket to draw from.

I have forced myself to begin writing when I've been utterly exhausted, when I've felt my soul as thin as a playing card...and somehow the activity of writing changes everything.
— JOYCE CAROL OATES

154. It Takes What It Takes

In 1947 Sinclair Lewis told Barnaby Conrad, his twenty-five-year-old personal secretary, that Conrad must write a novel based on the idea that John Wilkes Booth had escaped capture after assassinating Abraham Lincoln. He even had Conrad sign a contract stipulating that Lewis would get 30 percent of the deal. Sixty years and many books later, Conrad wrote *The Second Life of John Wilkes Booth*.

Stanley Kunitz was five years old when Halley's comet visited his hometown, Worcester, Massachusetts, in 1910. The memory of that night simmered for eighty-five years, and when he was almost ninety, he wrote the poem "Halley's Comet."

Creation is not simply a matter of a highly gifted person sitting down, thinking hard, and then writing, composing or painting something. There is an element of passivity, or dependence, even of humility in the creative process.

— ANTHONY STORR

155. Telling Family Secrets

When Maxine Hong Kingston first heard about her aunt who had been forced by her village to kill herself and her illegitimate child, she didn't know what to do with this wrenching story. Finally, as she was trying to write it, she thought, "I'm not going to publish this. I'm telling family secrets, I'm not going to publish this." Telling herself this gave her the freedom to put the story on paper and attempt to make it into art. After about twelve drafts she knew she had a resolution and a beautiful story. The story became the beginning of her book *The Woman Warrior*.

Most important of all I gave this woman's life a meaning. Then I felt, okay, now I can publish it.

— MAXINE HONG KINGSTON

156. Gratitude

At one point in her life, Maya Angelou thought she was going crazy. Terrified that she might do harm to herself and her young son, she went to a psychiatric hospital and tried to talk to a young doctor, but all she could do was cry. "How could this privileged young white man understand the heart of a black woman?" she wondered. So she left and went to the only person she thought could understand her, her mentor and voice teacher. When she told him how she felt, he said, "Sit down right here at this table, here is a yellow pad and here is a ballpoint pen. I want you to write down your blessings." She protested, and he told her to write down that she could hear, that she could see, and then to write that she could read. She finally followed his orders, and when she wrote the last line on the pad, she felt that "the agent of madness was routed."

Fifty years later — and twenty-five books and many poems, articles, plays, and speeches later — she is still writing on yellow pads and using ballpoint pens.

The essence of all beautiful art, all great art, is gratitude.
— FRIEDRICH NIETZSCHE

157. Dressed for Work

William Maxwell worked in his bathrobe and pajamas until about 12:30 PM. He thought it might be symbolic: "You can have me after I've got my trousers on but not before."

John Cheever owned only one suit when he started writing. He'd put the suit on every morning, take the elevator down to a basement room where he worked, take the suit off, hang it up, and write in his underwear. When he was finished for the day, he put the suit back on and took the elevator up to his apartment.

Caroline Leavitt wears red earrings when she writes. Alison Espach wrote her first novel wearing a lot of flannel, purple gloves with the fingers cut off, and wool socks from Ecuador. Francine Prose also wears flannel when she writes, her husband's red-and-black checked pajama pants with a T-shirt.

There's a photograph of Pablo Neruda writing at a formal desk, and this most passionate and romantic of poets is dressed in a suit and tie. He looks like the CEO of a successful company.

To publish a definitive collection of short stories in one's late 60s seems to me, as an American writer, a traditional and a dignified occasion, eclipsed in no way by the fact that a great many of the stories in my current collection were written in my underwear.

— JOHN CHEEVER

158. Winging It

Think of how much we just wing in life. Who on earth really knows how to be a parent when that baby arrives? You rely on instinct and act as if you know all about being a mother or father. You end up learning on the job. Who knows right off the bat how to cook breakfast or use a computer, or paint a wall or make love? One way or the other, you figure it out.

And who knows how to be a writer? You talk yourself into it; you act as if you know what you're doing. And if you keep going, eventually you will know what you're doing.

Sort of.

Writing is about hypnotizing yourself into believing in yourself, getting some work done.

— ANNE LAMOTT

159. What Would You Attempt?

A new coffee mug, a gift from a daughter, sits on my desk. It's black with white capital letters saying: "WHAT WOULD YOU ATTEMPT TO DO IF YOU KNEW YOU COULD NOT FAIL?"

Since I keep stumbling into things that have a huge built-in possibility for failure, I don't know how to answer this. But it does make me realize that if you're not writing and sending out your work because you're afraid of failure, you will never write, never be published. What have you ever done that didn't have the possibility of failure hidden in it?

Besides, failure is just another step going toward what you want to accomplish.

My reputation grows with every failure.
— GEORGE BERNARD SHAW

160. One-Hair Brushes

My artist friend Laura in Arizona, who sometimes gets the painter's version of writer's block, emails me that she just took a workshop in encaustic painting, which uses a medium of wax mixed with rich pigments and is done with heat, using torches, heat guns, hot plates, gouging, and melting. Previously she'd been working on icons, and she writes that this new medium is incredibly freeing and about as antithetical to icon painting as you can get: "No fussy one-hair brushes in sight!"

If you've been writing with the equivalent of a one-hair brush, maybe it's time to bring on the fire — the torches and the gouging and the melting. Loosen things up, get messy, let your writing get hot.

Technique alone is never enough. You have to have passion. Technique alone is just an embroidered potholder.

— RAYMOND CHANDLER

161. Dreams of Messy Rooms and Crazy Typewriters

Allan Gurganus's characters make cameo appearances in his dreams. John Nichols has used his dreams almost word for word in his writing. Isabel Allende has a recurring nightmare of a messy, disorganized house, rooms that she has to clean up, and the rooms never end. "Maybe I'm a writer because I'm desperately trying to clean up my mess," she writes.

Six years after Anne Rice had published *Interview with the Vampire*, she had a dream about the typewriter she'd written it on going crazy, "going and going and going and typing and typing and typing and it wouldn't stop." After the dream, she started her next book, and she writes, "That was the dream that said, 'Go to where the pain and the intensity and the fear is.' Because what I fear in writing is the safe decision. I want each book to be a risk."

I love Freud's term, the dreamwork, *because there is a kind of work involved in the making of the dream which is not dissimilar to the making of a story.*

— JOHN BARTH

162. Privacy, Privacy, Privacy

Most of us, if not all, have either experienced the violation of our journal or heard of someone who had it happen. Mine occurred early on — my mother read my pink diary with the useless little key and grounded me for about a thousand years. My brother read it too and sold excerpts at school. I learned my lesson.

Because the whole point of a journal or diary is that you're writing as if no one else will ever read it, make sure no one else ever reads it, unless you copy out passages and hand it to them. If your mother or significant other ransacks the house to find yours, you might consider looking for a calmer, more stable relationship.

The fear that someone might read a diary is the Censor's trump card....Privacy is key.

— ALEXANDRA JOHNSON

163. The Proper Training of a Writer

Maybe you don't have a college degree. Or maybe you have an MBA from Harvard. Or maybe you barely got through high school.

Do not use any of the above (including your MBA) as an excuse not to write. Very often our path to becoming a writer is messy and unpredictable and totally disconnected from formal education.

A writer needs three things: experience, observation, and imagination, any two of which, at times, any one of which, can supply the lack of the others.

— WILLIAM FAULKNER

164. Roadkill

One day there you are writing away with adrenaline flowing, dreams of the *New York Times Book Review* in your head, and then suddenly your work grinds to a halt and reads like roadkill. This can happen if you show it to the wrong person (reread entry 18, on your posse) — or if you simply run out of juice. Ellen Gilchrist says that when we write, we're trying to tell ourselves something important and we need to get to the end, to finish what we start.

Put it away for a while. Unlike roadkill, writing can come back to life.

Writing, I think, is a kind of debriefing.... There's a great deal more experience in our lives than we ever succeed in knowing. Writing is an attempt to acquire more of it.

— JOHN JEROME

165. Reading Aloud

When you read your work aloud, you can hear when the rhythm of your writing falters. Sometimes a run-on sentence isn't apparent until you find yourself stumbling over the words as you read.

Read it aloud to yourself because that's the only way to be sure the rhythms of the sentences are OK. Prose rhythms are too complex and subtle to be thought out — they can be got right only by ear.

— DIANA ATHILL

166. Blocks

In his poem "Weight Training," Brian Andreas writes about the giant block of whatever is most difficult for us and how we carry it around until we decide that this is what we want to do most, "& then it won't weigh / a thing anymore."

This poem can refer to a lot in life, but to writers it speaks clearly. Every time I read it, I vow to stop moaning about how hard writing is.

One morning at my desk, an essay I've had an idea about starts to unreel itself like a satin ribbon. Six hours later, I look up and realize I've been writing with ease.

— MARY KARR

167. Writing Space as a Metaphor

I once had a friend who was writing a play, who lived in a big house in Beverly Hills and was married to a well-known actor. She was struggling with taking the time and space necessary to do her work, but she kept writing. One day I saw a very small typewriter tucked away on her bedside table. She admitted that's where she worked, perched on the edge of her bed, taking up as little space as possible.

A woman must have money and a room of her own if she is to write fiction.

— VIRGINIA WOOLF

168. Hero Story

When he was fifty-one years old, Reynolds Price learned he had a ten-inch malignant tumor in his spine, and he believed that his happy life of writing and teaching was over. Surgery and radiation left him a paraplegic, in unspeakable pain, and not sure that he would survive. But he did survive and was able to manage his pain through hypnosis. He then finished a novel in progress (winning a National Book Award), continued to teach, and became even more prolific in the last twenty-five years of his life, writing poems, more fiction, and memoirs.

We need hero stories in every profession.

Writing is a fearsome but grand vocation — potentially healing but otherwise deadly. I wouldn't trade my life for the world.

— REYNOLDS PRICE

169. Just Do It

It never ends — how are you going to juggle your life, your family, your friends, your day job, your writing? A deadline simplifies things; you simply have to get on with it.

No deadline? Well, you're about halfway through the year of writing dangerously, so give yourself a six-month deadline.

Or take a writing class and get assignments. Family and friends tend to be more understanding when you tell them you have to finish an assignment for class than if you announce that you're going to write stories or poems all afternoon.

You also have permission to simply set your own deadline.

My country house is full of people, they never leave me alone; if only they would go away I could be a good writer.

— ANTON CHEKHOV

170. The Dangerous Place

In his famous essay "The Talent of the Room," Michael Ventura asks: "How long can you stay in that room? How many hours a day? How do you behave in that room? How often can you get back to it? How much fear (and, for that matter, how much elation) can you endure by yourself? How many years — how many YEARS — can you remain alone in a room?"

His premise is that the talent to spend long hours alone in a room is more important than writing talent, or style, or craft, or art.

If you can't handle the room, you can't handle the rest of it.

The writing life is essentially one of solitary confinement — if you can't deal with this you needn't apply.

— WILL SELF

171. Waiting

When asked if he ever suffered writer's block, Walker Percy recalled the one-word motto that Franz Kafka had on the wall over his bed: "*Warte*." *Wait*. Percy went on to say, "Oh, don't misunderstand me. I think you have to be sitting there. You have to 'wait' in good faith....I do think you have to have a routine and live up to it and then hope for the best."

A lot of writing consists of waiting around for the aquarium to settle so you can see the fish.

— ABIGAIL THOMAS

172. Hitting the Wall

In 1970 Patti Smith hit a wall. "I was both scattered and stymied, surrounded by unfinished songs and abandoned poems," she wrote in her memoir. "I would go as far as I could and hit a wall, my own imagined limitations. And then I met a fellow who gave me his secret, and it was pretty simple. When you hit a wall, just kick it in."

The source of that advice was Sam Shepard, then the biggest playwright off Broadway.

I feel like a bumper car. If I hit a wall, I'm backing up and going in another direction. And I've hit plenty of fucking walls in my career. But I'm not stopping. I think maybe that's my best quality: I just don't stop.

— CHER

173. Easy Plays

Sam Shepard said to Patti Smith one night, "Let's write a play." She told him that she didn't know anything about writing plays, and he said it was easy. He began it with describing her room on Twenty-Third Street in New York and then introduced his character. He gave her the typewriter and said it was her turn. She wrote her character. "Sam was right," she said. "It wasn't hard at all to write the play. We just told each other stories."

Well, okay, this was Sam Shepard and Patti Smith, after all. But when she got nervous about screwing up the rhythm in the dialogue, he gave her more good advice: "You can't make a mistake when you improvise....It's like drumming. If you miss a beat, just create another."

It's like improvising in jazz. You don't ask a jazz musician, "But what are you going to play?"

— JULIO CORTÁZAR

174. Another Way to Write a Play

Years before Sam Shepard said "Let's write a play" to Patti Smith, Tennessee Williams said more or less the same thing to Carson McCullers. She was visiting him in Nantucket after he sent her a fan letter inviting her to come visit. He was convinced that her books would make good theater, especially *The Member of the Wedding*, and suggested that she write a play. He then found a portable typewriter for her, and they sat at opposite ends of a long table, writing every day and passing a bottle of whiskey back and forth between them.

Don't bore the audience!...Just keep the thing going any way you can.

— Tennessee Williams

175. Telling about It

Sharon Olds wrote a poem about a photograph of her parents taken when they first met in college. In the poem she warns the beautiful couple not to get married, warns them of the terrible things that they'll do to each other, the suffering ahead, but then concludes, "I want to live." The final line of the poem speaks especially to writers: "Do what you are going to do, and I will tell about it."

We see people we have cherished, who are changed or dead, and we are reminded of our own fragility; our photographs serve as doorways into the past and its stories, and as cautionary omens.

— WILLIAM KITTREDGE

176. Writing on the High Wire

Sometimes writing is a high-wire act. You need to trust yourself, trust the wire you're balanced on, and trust the reasons that got you up there in the first place.

Every imaginative production must contain some element of risk.
— PAUL HORGAN

177. Lifelines

Anne Sexton, inspired by watching an educational TV show on how to write a sonnet, began to write poetry. She was a housewife at the time with two young daughters and in a fragile emotional state. She showed some of her poems to her psychiatrist, who encouraged her to keep writing. Writing poems, she said later, made her feel like she had a "purpose, a little cause, something to do with [her] life."

With a combination of madness and rare talent, she carved out a life as a poet for herself, and less than a decade later she won the Pulitzer Prize for her book of poetry *Live or Die*.

One of the jobs of poetry is to make the unbearable bearable, not by falsehood but by clear, concise confrontation.
— RICHARD WILBUR

178. The Duty of Poets and Writers

In William Faulkner's Nobel Prize speech in 1950, he said: "I believe that man will not merely endure: he will prevail. He is immortal, not because he alone among creatures has an inexhaustible voice, but because he has a soul, a spirit capable of compassion and sacrifice and endurance. The poet's, the writer's, duty is to write about these things. It is his privilege to help man endure by lifting his heart, by reminding him of the courage and honor and hope and pride and compassion and pity and sacrifice which have been the glory of his past. The poet's voice need not merely be the record of man, it can be one of the props, the pillars to help him endure and prevail."

Certainly morality should come first for writers, critics and everybody else. People who change tires. People in factories. They should always ask, is this moral? Not, will it sell?

— JOHN GARDNER

179. Figuring It Out

Years ago one of my students in a picture-book class handed me a twelve-page story entitled "The Year the Gypsies Came" and asked if I'd read it; she wasn't sure what it was. I read it, loved it, and told her it was going to be a novel. (It didn't take a genius to see this. It was all there — main character, setting, situation, and wonderful, quirky writing.) She said she didn't know how to write a novel. I told her she'd figure it out. A few years later I heard from her — she'd written the novel, and there was interest in it. Then silence, no one bought it, and she gave up on it.

Years later she went back to it, rewrote it, and finally sold it. *The Year the Gypsies Came* was published in the United States and the United Kingdom, and then Linzi Glass published two more novels.

I didn't believe I was capable of writing a novel but a year later I sat down and it poured out of me in ten months.

— Linzi Glass

180. The Authority of the Author

Who is the authority in your life? Who has the power?

Sam Keen points out that the words *authority* and *authorship* have the same root. "Whoever authors your story authorizes your actions," he writes.

This is your life, your story to write about. Create your own myth. You are the authority and you are the author.

Don't be satisfied with stories, how things have gone with others. Unfold your own myth.

— RUMI

181. Knowing Your Characters

Oddly, one of the best thoughts about how to treat your characters, whether real or fictional, with compassion, curiosity, and generosity comes from Abraham Lincoln. Commenting about someone he had just met, he said, "I don't like that man. I must get to know him better."

You can never know enough about your characters.

— SOMERSET MAUGHAM

182. Goofing Off

When I was working on an essay about my divorce, I figured it might help to read all my old journals about it, and since I write in my journal constantly when things aren't going well, I had a lot of material. I hadn't gone back to read this stuff for years, and I found the journals interesting in a car-crash sort of way. I sat around all afternoon reading pages of bad behavior, both his and mine. By the end of the day, I still didn't have a clue as to the shape of my essay, or what the themes were, or any of it. I just had a few chaotic paragraphs jotted down, but no clear path to the heart of it. I felt I had wasted most of the day, just goofed off. I took some deep breaths and tried to be calm about this. But, of course, I hadn't really wasted the day; it just felt like goofing off because I wasn't actually writing.

This can be one of the trickiest parts of being a writer, this need to fool around in order to be creative, and to be okay with that. So cut yourself some slack and trust that there's shape and meaning to what you want to write about and that if you take a lot of deep breaths and stay at your desk, you're going to discover it. Or so I try to tell myself.

Today is a dawdly day.

— JOHN STEINBECK

183. Running in the Dark

I used to love running in the dark. I couldn't see how far I had to go; I couldn't see other people, so I didn't get all self-conscious and wimpy; I felt free and invisible. This is what we try for in writing a first draft.

It's the old notion of blinding yourself so you can see. . . . I remove my glasses, pull a stocking cap down over my eyes, and type the first draft single spaced on the yellow paper in the actual and metaphorical darkness behind my closed eyes.

— KENT HARUF

184. Falling on Your Face

I have literally fallen on my face, besides doing it metaphorically and regularly on the page. A year ago, running in the dark, I tripped and fell. Not a stumble but a real fall on your face, with bloody knees and hands, and I thought: *Well, that's it. I have totally failed at this, and I don't have to run anymore. I can walk.* Which suddenly sounded very easy and pleasant to me.

But it was in the dark, after all, when I fell, and maybe only idiots run before sunrise on a cement path that has half-inch cracks rising up. So I had to revisit the whole thing, and after a year of walking sensibly, I went back to running.

This happens over and over again in writing.

My internal life as a writer has been a constant battle with the small, whispering voice (well, sometimes it shouts) that tells me I can't do it. This time, the voice taunts me, you will fall flat on your face.

— DANI SHAPIRO

185. Recharging

Sometimes to write you need to do more than just appear at your desk — you need to take care of the part of you that dreams and imagines and creates. Reading can usually do this for writers, but sometimes you also need to watch films, listen to music, go to an art museum, or see a play. Or just sit outside and soak up the sky.

Perhaps the most important and most difficult part of the writer's task is to revive his imagination every day during his working hours.

— PAUL HORGAN

186. Why Read?

If you're not reading, you're writing in a vacuum. You need books for inspiration, research, entertainment, as a model, and to remind you why you're writing in the first place. You need to love books. (If you don't, why write?) All the writers I know have a serious storage problem with their books.

I love the way real books smell and feel. I love to read the acknowledgments section to see if I know anybody mentioned, the dedication, the jacket endorsements, previous titles by the author, the index if there is one; I circle around a book for a while before I actually start reading. And when I teach, I have to have tangible books at hand, marked up with notes and festooned with Post-its.

But I also treasure ebooks when I travel; I took fourteen books to India this way, and for once my baggage was a manageable weight.

Reading usually precedes writing. And the impulse to write is almost always fired by reading. Reading, the love of reading, is what makes you dream of becoming a writer.

— SUSAN SONTAG

187: Owning Your Story

Whether it is true or out of your imagination, you own your story. You paid for it (trust me, you did). It's all yours. Use it, turn it inside out, cut it up, stretch it any way you please. Just remember: you own it. It's yours. Your version of what happened.

Suzanne Finnamore wrote a rage-fueled and hilariously honest memoir of her divorce, finishing it in seven years and "400 revisions." Her husband had left, telling her that she could write about this and it could probably make her a lot of money. One night shortly after he took off, Finnamore was sobbing and called Anne Lamott, who was an acquaintance, and told her that her husband had just left, telling her that she could write about the divorce. Lamott said, "YOU'RE GODDAMN RIGHT YOU CAN."

A writer's duty is to register what it is like for him or her to be in the world.

— ZADIE SMITH

188. An Army of Doubts

Doubts and fears can move in on you like an army — noisy, brandishing weapons, all suited up in official uniforms to intimidate you. It's just another version of the loud squawking bird on your shoulder or the critical voice in your head. Take cover and breathe deeply. When the smoke clears, resume writing.

I wish I had written more. I wish I had been more prolific. I wish I had had less fear of writing, more self-confidence, less terror of it.
— CYNTHIA OZICK

189. The Angle of the Wind

Rarely can a whole year go by in anyone's life without some kind of major disruption. A divorce, a death, an illness, moving, or losing a job. Brighter things can be disrupting too — a wedding, a new baby, graduations, major birthdays. All you can do during these times is to take notes.

I have pages and pages of notes describing an ICU room that R. was in when he had heart bypass surgery. There was a twofold benefit in this — note taking kept me from going crazy with anxiety, and if I ever write a scene that takes place in an ICU, I've got the details down.

It's like somebody taking a few moments out of being in the middle of a storm just to jot down the temperature, the angle of the wind....All very factual, flat, uninflected writing that just told the facts of what was happening.

— ALICE SEBOLD

190. The Telling Detail

A flyer appears in my mailbox. Fifi, a "skittish" Chihuahua, is missing: call Tanya at a phone number given. There's also this: "Wearing an aquamarine sweater."

Caress the detail, the divine detail.

— VLADIMIR NABOKOV

191. A Wasp and Its Nest

Jane Kenyon wrote a very short poem about a wasp "rising to its papery nest," trying to find a way into it, daubing at the nest, but it seemed "unable / to enter its own house." When I read the poem to my students without the title, they listen politely. And then I give them the title and read it again, and they make little noises and lightbulbs go off in their eyes. The title of the poem is "Not Writing."

Contrary to what many of you may imagine, a career in letters is not without its drawbacks — chief among them the unpleasant fact that one is frequently called upon to sit down and write.

— FRAN LEBOWITZ

192. About Craft

You can get guidelines for fiction and nonfiction; you can be steered toward beautiful writing with the hope that you'll be inspired and understand craft in a way that can't always be articulated. But neither I nor any teacher has a neat chart for how to do this.

Craft has to do with rewriting, with honing the words down to story and emotion. Craft is about shifting your gaze from your own belly button to the world at large. It's like being a carpenter; you cut and you sand and you polish. It's about realizing that you will never, ever stop learning your craft.

Nobody taught me lessons in craft as such. It was more a question of learning to be a good reader of my own work, and of other people's work as well.

— TOBIAS WOLFF

193. Milkweed and Forsythia

Mark Doty says that the more we can name of what we see and the more words we have for it, the more we care and the less we are likely to destroy what we see. He uses as an example the generic word *meadow* — and believes we'll care more if the meadow is bulldozed for a strip mall if we know "those tall flat-leaved spires are milkweed, upon which the monarchs have flown two thousand miles to feed." Natalie Goldberg says, "When we know the name of something, it brings us closer to the ground. It takes the blur out of our mind; it connects us to the earth. If I walk down the street and see 'dogwood,' 'forsythia,' I feel more friendly toward the environment."

It takes more energy to do this, both mental and emotional. But specificity makes you a better writer.

I believe in the power and mystery of naming things. Language has the capacity to transform our cells, rearrange our learned patterns of behavior, and redirect our thinking. I believe in naming what's right in front of us because that is often what is most invisible.

— EVE ENSLER

194. Cake and Architecture

My students want to know about structure, as if I can pull out a blueprint or a recipe for them: "Okay, now do this and that — be sure to include x, add a little y, and finish up with z — and voilà, you'll have a poem, an essay, a novel." This works for buildings and cakes, but not so much for poetry and stories.

I can offer examples of structure, how others pulled it off for their books. I can suggest that your poem doesn't have to be linear but can make leaps and somersaults; I can suggest that your essay might circle around at the end to something you introduced in the first paragraph; and I can make all kinds of suggestions for tenses and points of view in fiction. But the bottom line is this: they are simply suggestions — you must find your own structure. And you will.

I don't believe stories are told from A to Z anymore, or if they are, they become very ponderous.

— Michael Ondaatje

195. One of the Worst Things a Writer Can Do

Here's something you want to think twice about: throwing away your essay or fiction or memoir because you hate it. You can hide it from view on your computer, stash a hard copy in a closet — but don't destroy it. Because sometimes it's simply impossible to judge your own work. Sometimes all you need is time. The wastepaper basket is not always a writer's best friend.

John Banville, author of thirteen much-acclaimed books, was asked in an interview if he likes his books, and he replied: "No, I hate them all. With a deep, abiding hatred. And embarrassment. I have a fantasy that I'm walking past Brentano's or wherever and I click my fingers and all my books on the shelves go blank. The covers are still there but all the pages are blank. And then I can start again and get it right." (This is the same John Banville who won the Booker Prize, was shortlisted again for the Booker, and won the Franz Kafka Prize and the Irish Book Award.)

When it's finally in print, you're delivered — you don't ever have to look at it again. It's too late to worry about its failings.
— EUDORA WELTY

196. Clutter as a Metaphor

When I finish a draft of a book, I always clear up the clutter, the chaos and mess, in my office. As I write the second draft, the clutter all comes back. It's a living metaphor. I'm also dealing with the clutter/mess/chaos of my thoughts and writing.

When I started writing, I had a little file box full of my work that I'd take out at 1:00 every afternoon when my babies were napping. I'd write for an hour at the kitchen table and then put my stories back in the file box and hide the box. This was also a metaphor.

Seeing the value of metaphor in your life, talking about the value of metaphor, that's what's important.

— CLIVE BARKER

197. Very Personal Clutter

In William Zinsser's book *On Writing Well*, there's a chapter on clutter that every writer should read. The book was published in 1976, but Zinsser's examples of word clutter are still being used ("a personal friend of mine," "it is interesting to note," "for the reason that," etc.). Since then, word clutter has grown by leaps and bounds via the Internet, or as he said in 1976, "New varieties sprout overnight, and by noon they are part of American speech."

When you rewrite, get rid of the clutter. Simplify. Of course a friend is personal. Just tell us something; don't do the interesting note introduction. And the word *because* can eliminate four words you don't need.

Prune it ruthlessly. Be grateful for everything that you can throw away.... Can any thought be expressed with more economy? Is anything pompous or pretentious or faddish? Are you hanging on to something useless just because you think it's beautiful?
— WILLIAM ZINSSER

198. Some Writers' Beginnings

For every Stephen King, whose mother gave him their food money for postage so he could send his stories out to publishers at age twelve, there's a Chris Abani, whose father hated the idea of his writing so much that he burned the first draft of his son's first manuscript.

Or the stalwart Francine du Plessix Gray (Charles Olson's beleaguered student), who was told at age eight by her father that she was writing pathetic dribble and should never write again. (She didn't try fiction for over thirty years.) Parents disparage their children's writing at their own peril. In the acknowledgments section of *This Boy's Life*, Tobias Wolff writes that his stepfather used to say that what Wolff didn't know could fill a book. "Well, here's the book," Wolff writes.

I didn't give up, largely because of my father's faith in me.

— ANNE LAMOTT

199. Waiting in the Marble

When Wally Lamb discusses teaching writing to inmates in a correctional institution, he quotes Michelangelo: "I saw the angel in the marble and carved until I set him free." He calls his students, and himself, damaged angels in waiting "who have the potential to sculpt our best selves with the aid of paper and pen."

Everyone, *everyone*, has an angel waiting inside the marble. I know this from the experience I had working with people who were dealing with cancer. For years I conducted a writing workshop for a cancer support group, and the people who came to my workshop wanted to write as therapy. They were not there to become writers, but each and every one of them wrote toward their angel and found themselves on paper.

Which of us is so self-aware that we could not reveal ourselves more deeply by reflecting on our lives with fingertips on the keyboard?

— WALLY LAMB

200. Write What You Read

If you read and love detective novels, maybe that's what you should be writing. Or if you read romance novels — that might be your genre. One of my daughters was a closet romance reader in college ("mind candy" she called it). I'd never read one, but she told me how popular they were, how many were published each month. So we decided to become the famous mother-and-daughter team of romance authors; we'd write them together, and we'd make tons of money and have a lot of fun doing it.

She was on spring break at the time, so we hung around the house, wrote three chapters and a plot outline in a week, and had a marvelous time. I came up with a road-trip plot with a lot of humor. (I have to admit that I included a stop for our heroine in Intercourse, Pennsylvania, that we thought was hilarious.) The problem, of course, was that these novels don't normally have a lot of humor. They are not supposed to have hilarious scenes in them. And possibly it showed that I had never read anything in this genre. It was quickly rejected by all the publishers we sent it to, and our days of becoming the wealthy queens of romance ended abruptly.

What we want in a nutshell: Talented, dedicated authors who are savvy about the romance genre and its readers.

— Harlequin Website,
"How to Write the Perfect Romance!"

201. Questions

Tobias Wolff doesn't assign writing exercises to his students. "I think each time out should be a swing for the fences," he says. Base-running drills they can do on their own time. What's important and what he asks his students is this: "What is there in the necessities of this particular character that produces this narrative? What has mattered to the writer in the writing of this story?"

When I give five-minute exercises in class, I tell my students to use them for their own selfish purposes — for either warming up or to find something new for their story or essay.

I like worrying about the folks I write about. I want to know if everything's gonna turn out OK for them. I want to show what can happen when we err, and when we "do the right thing," because as they say no matter what you do, sometimes, "shit happens."

— TERRY McMILLAN

202. On Planning and Plotting

You know the saying about how God laughs when you make plans? This holds especially true for writers. Now I do know a few writers who come up with meticulously planned outlines before starting a book, and it works wonderfully for them; but for many of us an outline is as mysterious and difficult as an algebra equation. We have to just jump in and see what happens.

How do I know what I think until I see what I say?

— E. M. FORSTER

203. Ignoring the Snark

A writer suggested in a prominent publication that there are too many people writing and publishing memoirs, and asked who wants to read another book about owning a crazy dog, losing weight, depression, cancer, trying to adopt, etc.

Ignore snarky articles like this. If you went through a difficult experience and came out on the other side and can write about it in clear, specific prose, maybe with a little humor too, and we can take that journey with you and learn something — you've got to write your book or your essay.

The snark in these articles is just crankiness and an attempt at being cool. Don't let it put a damper on your fire. Keep writing.

These are the facts, my friend, and I must have faith in them.

— CICERO

204. A Writer's Rant

"I'm here again with nothing to say....I haven't written in more than a week. Forgive me, O Muse, for being absent without leave. Maybe it's the Prozac. Maybe it's the rain. Maybe it's because I'm too damn vain. Can't I put down simple words and send them out the door? Does it matter how they're dressed? Does it matter if they're poor?"

The above appeared in Sy Safransky's column in the literary magazine he edits, the *Sun*. But then he went on, as he always does, to get out of his own angst. On occasion a reader has written in to suggest that he lighten up and pull himself together, but I frankly love to read that someone who produces a successful literary magazine and bares his heart to the world has the same problem I do getting words out the door.

Did I expect the God of Writing to invite me up to his penthouse suite, sweep all the crap off his desk, and offer me a seat?

— Sy Safransky

205. Saving Trees

I have a friend who talks about saving the trees and asks why I have to keep encouraging people to write and use up all that paper. Because I think everybody can write *something*, I tell him. And furthermore they *need* to write whatever that something is. Maybe it's a self-published collection of love letters to their kids, or recipes. Maybe it's the great American novel or a memoir that will jolt the literary world. Or maybe it's one short poem or an essay. But it needs to be written.

This is what Brenda Ueland had to say about the reason to exercise your creative power: "Because there is nothing that makes people so generous, joyful, lively, bold and compassionate, so indifferent to fighting and the accumulation of objects and money."

I am sitting here, my thoughts carrying me around the world and within myself, trying to record the voyage on paper....I want to write about moments I regard as gifts, good moments and bad moments.

— LIV ULLMANN

206. The Meaning of Meaning

Mihaly Csikszentmihalyi says that one of the definitions of the word *meaning* is "significance" — the assumption that events are linked to each other toward an ultimate goal, that there's order and connection to what happens to us. Which is not always the case in the mess of everyday life. This is why we love plots in fiction and memoirs that teach us how life can work out and not stay mired in a stew of meaninglessness and craziness.

People who find their lives meaningful usually have a goal that is challenging enough to take up all their energies, a goal that can give significance to their lives.

— MIHALY CSIKSZENTMIHALYI

207. Owning "I"

Some of my students haul into class all the rules and regulations they learned in grade-school English. One rule is that you never start a paragraph with "I." I'm not sure anymore the reason behind this — false modesty? I have no idea how you go about writing personal nonfiction without using the word "I," owning "I," and using it as much as you please.

We really possess nothing on this earth but the power to say I.
— SIMONE WEIL

208. Once upon a Time

We can get so into our own feelings that all we want to deal with are the high points, the arias, not the heavy lifting that story requires — scene setting, event and consequence, pace, tension, escalating action. Patience and detail are required to tell a story, whether made-up or true. The desire to hear a story is basic and primitive, but it takes time to set it up.

A story can take you through a whole process of searching, seeking, confronting, through conflicts, and then to a resolution. As the storyteller and listener, we go through a story together.
— Maxine Hong Kingston

209. Your Own Watcher

Gail Godwin wrote an essay about her version of the critic on your shoulder entitled "The Watcher at the Gates" for an op-ed page. She had suggestions for outwitting the watcher: pretend you're just writing a letter, write when you're very tired, write in purple ink on a credit card statement, write whatever comes into your mind while waiting for the kettle to boil.

On a very bad day she wrote a letter to her watcher, asking him what it was that he was so afraid she'd do. Then she held the pen for him so he could reply. "Fail," he wrote back.

It is amazing the lengths a Watcher will go to to keep you from pursuing the flow of your imagination.

— GAIL GODWIN

210. A Vocation

We can overthink things too much. Again (and again): you're a writer if you write. Sitting around clutching your hands together and *wanting* to be a writer just leads you to general despair and a desire to eat chocolate or drink wine.

Natalia Ginzburg opens her elegant essay "My Vocation" with these lines: "My vocation is to write and I have known this for a long time. I hope I won't be misunderstood; I know nothing about the value of the things I am able to write. I know that writing is my vocation."

Don't judge yourself. Just follow your vocation and write.

If a vocation is as much the work that chooses you as the work you choose, then I knew from that time on that my vocation was, for better or worse, to involve that searching for, and treasuring, and telling of secrets which is what the real business of words is all about.

— FREDERICK BUECHNER

211. A Different Perspective

If you're writing on a computer, be sure to print out at intervals — not only to avoid losing your work through a technical disaster but also to make notes on your manuscript. Writing notes on real paper gives you a different perspective. Hitting the Delete button can be too easy.

Part of being a writer is the capacity to live with imperfection, particularly as a work of fiction first takes shape.

— THOMAS FARBER

212. Four Things That Never Change

Here are four things I learn over and over every time I teach a creative writing class, workshop, or retreat:

1. Of the people who come to writing workshops, 99.9 percent are insecure about their writing.
2. Five-minute writing exercises are the best way for people to jump into whatever they're nervous about writing.
3. Everybody has a story to tell.
4. People who are serious about writing let down their guard in a very short time.

Art is concerned with production.

— ARISTOTLE

213. Songs, Not Answers

A student sends me a card with a Chinese proverb: "The bird does not sing because it has an answer; it sings because it has a song."

You don't need to write the answers. You just need to write your story.

Those hours of writing had a shape, a fullness, and a solidity that ordinary hours did not have. They were round and full, like fruit.
— KATHARINE BUTLER HATHAWAY

214. Questions of Life

The final paragraph of Caroline Knapp's memoir about redefining her world after she quit drinking, lost both her parents, and fell in love with a dog doesn't provide a conclusion but literally asks questions: "What makes you feel empty and what makes you feel full? Who, or what, makes you feel connected or soothed or joyful? How much companionship do you need, and how much solitude? What feels right and what feels like enough?" Her dog, Lucille, couldn't answer the questions for her, but Knapp realized Lucille was gently pulling her forward toward the answers.

For writers, questions are always the starting place.

All the books are questions for me. I write them because I didn't know something.

— TONI MORRISON

215. Hard Truth

Dorothy Allison wrote *Two or Three Things I Know for Sure* as a performance piece and then revised it for publication. In it she compares a story to a disguise, a razor, or "a tool that changes every time it is used and sometimes becomes something other than we intended." And she says that the use of fiction "in a world of hard truth...can be a harder piece of truth."

The paradox of fiction: it can be more true than the "real" story.

Two or three things I know for sure, and one of them is what it means to have no loved version of your life but the one you make.
— DOROTHY ALLISON

216. Be Silly, Sound Stupid, and Spill the Beans

Stop clinging to that wall with your fingernails, trying to do this right (if indeed that's how your writing feels). Sometimes we just have to write toward what we fear the most: boring our readers; sounding silly; revealing too much; or sounding too emotional, sentimental, or simply dumb. Go for it — be silly, sound stupid, and/or spill the beans. I fear being boring so much that sometimes I have to give myself an assignment to write the most boring page ever committed to paper, and then I get over myself and my boringness and get back to writing the story.

If you are afraid of being sentimental, say, for heaven's sake be as sentimental as you can or feel like being! Then you will probably pass through to the other side.

— Brenda Ueland

217. The Wave of the Future Passing You By

I had the privilege of working with an editor who was known in children's publishing as a "legend." I tell you about this because the editor, Margaret K. McElderry, whose books won many Caldecott and Newbery Medals (one memorable year her books won both medals), had not been, shall we say, overly encouraged in her early career or even in midcareer. When she was a senior in college, she was told that she had no future in publishing. Years later, when she was head of the children's department at Harcourt, Brace, her boss told her, "The wave of the future has passed you by," and fired her. Margaret got another job and went on to win awards and to edit and publish for over thirty more years after that, working into her nineties with enormous energy and enthusiasm and success.

If you don't catch them young, you won't have any adult readers.
— MARGARET K. McELDERRY

218. Looking for Something in the Dark

Some writers describe rooms without windows, or fumbling in the dark, when they talk about trying to write. In March 1970 James Salter wrote to his friend Robert Phelps: "All week I've tried to write a story. I know everything about it, I can almost read it and yet I can't seem to write a single paragraph which interests me. It's like looking for something in the dark, there's such a huge amount of chance in writing."

A few days later Robert Phelps writes back: "I haven't been able to write anything for two months. Or rather, I write and write but it's 'fiction.' I don't believe what I'm saying.... I can't seem to forget myself long enough to get something written."

But a few months later here's Salter back up to speed: "We must consume whole worlds to write a single sentence and yet we never use up a part of what is available. I love the infinities, the endlessness involved."

Writing a first draft is like groping one's way into a dark room, or overhearing a faint conversation, or telling a joke whose punch line you've forgotten.

— TED SOLOTAROFF

219. Our Baggage

Talking about audiences who came to see a play she was in, Vanessa Redgrave said: "We all come to the theater with baggage. The baggage of our daily lives, the baggage of our problems, the baggage of our tragedies, the baggage of being tired. It doesn't matter what age you are, but if our hearts get opened and released — well, that's what theater can do."

Our readers come with baggage too, and it's our job as writers to open their hearts.

All great artists draw from the same resource: the human heart, which tells us all that we are more alike than we are unalike.

— MAYA ANGELOU

220. Tomatoes

Let's say you're growing tomatoes. Some of you will keep a very tidy garden, and you'll secure your plants on poles with little wire twists, feed and water your tomatoes regularly, and be alert for pests who want to eat them. Finally one warm summer day you'll harvest some delicious tomatoes.

Others of you will not be so tidy, and things might get out of control. Maybe your vines will creep where they're not supposed to, the poles will collapse, a few evil green worms will appear and scare the daylights out of you, and you'll have a tomato jungle on your hands. But tomato plants are hardy, and one warm summer day you'll harvest some delicious tomatoes.

This is not unlike writing stories. Stories don't die easily, and we all go about writing them in our own way.

I would like to be like the person who raises vegetables. I don't have to run out and show someone passing in the street how good my onions are....They're just growing, that's all....Nothing especially remarkable.

— WILLIAM STAFFORD

221. Losing Your Eye

I am not a good photographer. R., who's a real photographer, says that if I were an assassin, I'd be shooting bystanders. However, last year I acquired a phone with a camera that manages to take wonderful photographs no matter how inept I am. For the first few weeks that I owned this phone camera, I did little writing; I just took pictures.

Here's the beauty of a camera: *you don't have to come up with words for what you're looking at.* I realized I was burned out from trying to describe things — trees, cows, cats, sky, rooms, action, faces. I had temporarily lost the words to make things visible.

R. tells me that photographers can temporarily lose their eye.

Maybe another angle is needed sometimes. When we're burned out from writing, we can photograph or draw, look at the world in a different way, and photographers could try writing what they see.

A camera is a tool for learning how to see without a camera.
— Dorothea Lange

222. Origins of a Bestseller

Umberto Eco was writing scholarly books on how cultures communicate with signs and symbols, when a publishing friend told him about an anthology of detective stories he wanted to publish. Eco said to his friend, "[There's] no way I could write a detective story, but if I ever did write one it would be a five-hundred-page book with medieval monks." That night Eco made a list of names for fictional medieval monks and eventually began writing a murder mystery including the monks. A few years later *The Name of the Rose* became an international bestseller.

Those things about which we cannot theorize, we must narrate.

— Umberto Eco

223. LOL

Humor can be wit, irony, pushing truth to the edges, slapstick, satire, exaggeration, absurdity, and, if you're under the age of twelve, fart jokes.

On the beach one morning I saw a sign that had previously been posted on the chain-link fence that protected a construction area where they were putting up new beach bathrooms. Someone had ripped it off the fence, and it was now lying in the sand. The sign read, "Thank you for your patience." I found this hysterically funny, but you may not find it even remotely amusing. This is why humor is so difficult to pull off, and very personal, but if you can make a reader laugh or even smile, it is a rare and marvelous thing to do.

Nicholson Baker wanted to be a writer ever since he found his mother laughing out loud over an essay about golf by John Updike. "Nothing is more impressive," Baker said, "than the sight of a complex person suddenly ripping out a laugh over some words in a serious book or periodical.... Here was Updike making people happy. That was obviously something to be proud of."

Humor is one of the hardest things to define, very hard.... You have it or you don't.

— HEINRICH BÖLL

224. Sicker, Not Richer

Lorrie Moore received a letter from a friend saying that he'd been following and enjoying her work, and that it was "getting better: deeper and richer." On closer examination she realized that he'd written "sicker," not "richer." Which led her to wonder about what writers and artists were supposed to do, and what art was supposed to be about, and "whether it could possibly include some aesthetics of sickness." In an essay about this, she lists her childhood obsessions, such as cutting little bows, lace flowers, etc., off her dresses, collecting shiny objects like a magpie, drawing songs as she listened to them, and having a strange crush on Bill Bixby.

At the end of her essay, she quotes William Carlos Williams and says, "He was a doctor. So presumably he knew about *sicker* and *better* and how they are often quite close."

When we use writing to create a story, like it or not a kind of toxin that lies deep down in all humanity rises to the surface.

— HARUKI MURAKAMI

225. Writing as If

No one (believe me, *no one*) will take you seriously as a writer until you take yourself seriously. And even then, one or two grumpy people in your acquaintance may wonder aloud over all the time you have to spend sequestered with your computer.

Publishing something you've written may give you a momentary bump of self-esteem — it will certainly give you hope — but publishing won't give you the supreme and secure knowledge that YOU ARE A WRITER.

Sometimes, to get through the doubt, you just have to proceed *as if* you're a writer.

Whatever time you decide to write, own that time. Shut the door and don't communicate with the outside world. If you end up staring at the blank screen of your computer, wondering what the hell you're going to write about, that's fine. It's what writers do.

Only there, in the room with closed doors and the blinds drawn against the seductive outdoors, with the phone turned off, will anything good or useful come to you.

— DORIS GRUMBACH

226. Lost and Found

Some days you have your writing voice. Whatever yours is —
funny, thoughtful, sassy, tough, tender — it's alive on the page
and right for your story. Then suddenly one day it goes flat as a
bad textbook, or phony and forced. The only way to find your
voice again is to keep writing. Have faith; it'll come back.

*I soon discovered that if I wanted to speak truthfully in this memoir
— that I, without cynicism or sentiment — I had to find a tone of
voice normally not mine. The one I habitually lived with wouldn't
do at all: it whined, it grated, it accused; above all, it accused.*

— VIVIAN GORNICK

227. Taking a Break

Nelson, in his doggy wisdom, knows it's not good to hunch over a bright little screen for hours and hours at a time, not moving. He puts his paws on my knees and begs me to take a break.

Breaks are necessary, of course; we need to move, exercise.

Sometimes a break of a week or more is also necessary when you're working intensely on a book or even on a short piece. Gaining perspective on your own work is like studying a painting with your nose pressed up against the canvas. Sometimes it helps to switch to another writing project and let things rest.

Writing calls on unused muscles and involves solitude and immobility.

— DOROTHEA BRANDE

228. Five Feet of Failure

When I think of Thomas Edison and his one thousand steps (not failures but *steps*) to success, I think of the many, many steps — all the drafts — it takes to complete a novel. I used to save all of mine, and one day I carted the drafts of my second novel — just published — into class, thinking that it would inspire my students. (*Look how I struggled! But look, it turned into a published book!*) They were not inspired. Instead, they appeared profoundly depressed by the sight of my five-foot-tall stack of failed drafts.

Some things are best left to the imagination.

The wastepaper basket is a writer's best friend.
— Isaac Bashevis Singer

229. One Writer's Tools

Fran Lebowitz's famous case of writer's block (she has two long overdue, unfinished books) is now simply a fact, but when she does write, she writes with a pen on a legal pad. A friend showed her an iPad once and told her how easy it was to use. She thought: "I'm going to wait until it really works because at the point when it really works, it's going to be a pad of paper. As soon as it becomes a yellow legal pad, I'm set."

I write in longhand, and I write in very beautiful notebooks and with very beautiful pens.... If I write a page a day, I'm lucky.
— EDMUND WHITE

230. My Direct Line

I did one thing that was brilliant when I started writing: I ordered my own phone line. My personal line was a financial extravagance at that point in my life, but it enabled me to not answer the family phone (which rang all the time) when I was writing. I had a husband traveling the freeways every day, small children in school, and parents in another state, so I had to be available by phone in case there was an emergency; and having my own private, unlisted number solved the problem. Of course, caller ID and cell phones now solve the problem for everybody, so you're going to have to find another way to do something brilliant for your writing career. But I made a statement with my phone line. The layer of privacy the phone gave me said that my writing was important. It was my work number; only my family and my daughters' school had it. It made me feel like a professional person.

We have to make myths out of our lives.

— MAY SARTON

231. Obsession

Sometimes you're just slogging along at your desk, putting in the time, uninspired, and then suddenly your story takes off with everything but sirens blasting. And you forget to eat, to shower — and who cares about newspapers and what's going on in the rest of the world? You're into your own world; the concept of time has disappeared. This can be productive and exhilarating. You can make great leaps and bounds with your work. Though if you're living with other people, they may snipe at you for becoming a workaholic.

There was a cartoon in the *New Yorker* years ago that I saved because of some sniping from people I lived with. The sky outside the window in the cartoon is dark, and an artist stands at his easel shouting at his wife: "Workaholic? Brokers and salesmen are workaholics. Artists are obsessed. There's a difference."

There's nothing like the burn you get when it's going well, when things feel incandescent in your writing.

— THOMAS McGUANE

232. Magic Caves

My friend Billy Mernit has made his office into what he calls his "cave": books covering three walls, and tiny blue lights, like runway lights, along the shelves; a giant wooden paper clip that reads "Artist at Work," which belonged to his late, beloved father; music that he says helps to make his mind move; and cats lounging on his orderly desk. I love to think of him writing in there.

Amy Tan surrounds herself with objects that have history for her — bowls and boxes, old books. Rita Dove writes in the silence of her cabin, standing up at a desk with a lit candle. In Montana, Thomas McGuane writes in a remodeled bunkhouse.

Sometimes, picturing other writers at work, sitting alone in their caves and cabins, surrounded by things they love, can comfort us with the knowledge that we're not the only ones sitting alone in a room, going down that runway, trying to find some magic in our stories.

I imagine the people who once turned the pages or rubbed their palms on the surfaces. While they were thinking — thinking what?

— AMY TAN

233. The Face on the Wall

William Styron wrote about having writer's block as "creative impotence...struggling with the obdurate word, with the intransigent paragraph, with the hopelessly unyielding sentence, word, comma." Its effect? "One wants to give it all up and go to Peru and fish sardines...anything but write."

He didn't go to Peru to fish for sardines. Instead, one morning he woke in a half-dream state and saw on his bedroom wall the face of a girl, a Polish refugee he had met briefly years before who had a concentration camp tattoo on her arm. Her name was Sophie. This vision caused him to begin writing *Sophie's Choice*.

It is this kind of mystery, rather than any hard definition of what writing is, that makes writing such an enormously fascinating and challenging, and in the end, I hope, triumphant human occupation.
— WILLIAM STYRON

234. John Hersey and His Mother

Accepting a literary award at a writer's conference years ago, John Hersey spoke about what writing teachers can offer students. How they can help new writers understand "what it means to live by and for writing" and how important it is to understand the attitudes that working writers have toward their work, how they go about it, their goals and beliefs, where and how they find their material and shape it. And also how writers must learn to read for both pleasure and craft, "constantly watching the author's hand."

Long before I ever read John Hersey, I knew Mrs. Hersey, his mother, the librarian at the Briarcliff Public Library. She was a large, friendly woman, and I wish I could go back in time and ask her a hundred questions about her son John. What it meant to him to live by and for writing. But I was in grade school, checking out Nancy Drew books every week, and had no idea who he was.

Only the masters, finally, can teach writing; only the student herself or himself, by doing, by trial and error, can learn, can find his or her appropriate and uniquely personal voice in words.

— John Hersey

235. Attitude

At age fifty, Dominick Dunne was working in Hollywood as a successful producer but felt discontented; what he really wanted to do was write. So he went to a cabin in the woods in Oregon, worked very, very hard for a long time, and came up with his first novel. It was published and got a terrible review in the *New York Times*. "They just savaged it," Dunne said years later, adding that it was just as hard to write a bad book as a good one. But then he thought to himself: "Listen, I'm fifty-three years old and I wrote a book and I got a book published by Simon & Schuster and by god it got reviewed in the *New York Times*!"

His next book was a bestseller.

What matters is the process: the experience of shaping that artwork. The viewers' concerns are not your concerns (although it's dangerously easy to adopt their attitudes).... Your job is to learn to work on your work.

— DAVID BAYLES and TED ORLAND, *Art & Fear*

236. Stealing

Writers steal. Which is different from plagiarizing. We don't copy the words verbatim; we copy the technique. There's a well-known Natalia Ginzburg essay entitled "He and I" in which she goes back and forth between, on the one hand, what her husband loves, feels, says, and can do and, on the other, what she loves, feels, says, and can do. A lot of the writers I know who teach the personal essay give this as an exercise to their students. In fact, once I stole this technique for an essay of my own.

Recently in class I read an essay to my students with the great opening line "Here is what you should know about my father." It was immediately stolen to wonderful effect by a student who began his essay, "Here's what you should know if you're a dog in Los Angeles."

I shamelessly steal ideas, devices, techniques, methodology, good habits from everybody I can find. I think the best way to teach yourself to write is by reading, and reading not for the meaning but for how-did-the-guy-get-that-effect. And I do it all the time.

— TONY HILLERMAN

237. Why They Write

"Guilt is the thing that really drives me," says Harlan Coben. "Every day that I'm not writing I hear a mother's voice in my head: 'Why aren't you writing that book?' People ask what my hobbies are. I don't have hobbies. I don't because when I'm doing anything else, I feel like I'm supposed to be writing."

Dani Shapiro's motivation for writing is connection. "To say: this is me, my truth, my world."

Jayne Anne Phillips's short answer to why she writes is: "I don't know why and I hope I never find out."

"The only time I know the truth is when it reveals itself at the point of my pen," Jean Malaquais told Norman Mailer.

I write entirely to find out what I'm thinking, what I'm looking at, what I see and what it means.

— Joan Didion

238. Revising

My agent once told me to stop rewriting a novel that had just sold. It had a publisher, it had been edited, and I was driving everybody nuts with my last-minute revisions. Months later, when I received published copies of the book, I added a number of changes to the first chapter in one copy with a pen and mailed it off to my agent.

Revisions can be one of the pure joys of writing. You've done all the heavy lifting; now you can polish.

I read that Marianne Moore wouldn't sign copies of her poetry books until she had made what she thought were necessary corrections.

I often wish that I could have twenty years more, to take them down from the shelf one by one, and write them over.

— WASHINGTON IRVING

239. The Good and the Bad

William Saroyan once got a letter from one of his readers asking, "How could you write so much good stuff and still write so much bad stuff?"

Fifteen years ago a friend who had published many novels and won many awards sent me the first draft of the opening chapter of a new novel. My friend was a wonderful writer, but she had written a chapter that wasn't very good. She was also smart and realized exactly where she had gone off track when I gave her some feedback. "Thank God we don't have printing presses at home and can't publish this stuff ourselves!" she said.

Of course now, heaven help us, with Internet publishing we can, so more than ever we need our posse, people who know our best work and can tell us when what we write isn't our best.

Sometimes people don't like what you've done because it is terrible.
— EDWARD ALBEE

240. Write and/or Die

When Mary Karr was working on her third memoir, she threw out five hundred pages of the manuscript, leaving just the early chapters. Then a few years later she threw out another five hundred pages. "I was nearing my deadline," she said, "and my tit was in the wringer timewise. A sane person might've bargained with my publisher for more time, but I didn't. It was as if God were saying, You're in this now: do it. Which, by the way, my publisher said too."

She has a couple of writer friends she calls when she's going through a bad time with her writing. One of them, Don DeLillo, sent her a postcard after she called.

"Write or Die," he wrote on it. She sent one back to him that said, "Write and Die."

Writers when they're writing live in a spooky, clamorous silence, a state somewhat like the advanced stages of prayer but without prayer's calming benefits.

— JOY WILLIAMS

241. Cliffs and Icebergs

Icebergs and cliff edges are popular metaphors for writers — dangerous, precarious, cold. I can't think of any writers who compare writing to a romp through warm, flowering meadows.

Peter Carey compared writing fiction to standing on the edge of a cliff: "This is especially true of the first draft. Every day you're making up the earth you're going to stand on."

Anne Carson remembered a sentence for a poem "driving at [her] in the dark like a glacier." Carson said, "I felt like a ship going toward the South Pole and then all of a sudden a glacier comes zooming out of the dark, and I just took it down."

Ernest Hemingway had his iceberg theory (also known as the theory of omission): "If a writer of prose knows enough of what he is writing about he may omit things that he knows.... The dignity of movement of an ice-berg is due to only one-eighth of it being above water."

Every morning I jump out of bed and step on a landmine. The landmine is me. After the explosion, I spend the rest of the day putting the pieces together.

— RAY BRADBURY

242. The Blank Page

What is the worst thing that can happen when you sit down to write? A blank page, a blank screen? There will always be a blank page or screen; you'll face it every day of your writing life no matter how much you write and publish. There will be that blank space to cover with words, with thoughts, with stories, every single day. And if you turn away from it, if you don't go near it, it will still be in your mind — that space to fill.

This is terrifying — and it can also be thrilling.

It becomes a choice between certainty and uncertainty. And curiously, uncertainty is the comforting choice.
— DAVID BAYLES and TED ORLAND, *Art & Fear*

243. Stepping Up to the Plate

Thomas McGuane says that all writers with a good idea for a book "have this same terrified subdued feeling, which is a reluctant desire to step up to the plate for better or worse."

How many potentially great books are hidden away in desk drawers? How many poems and stories were not written because someone was afraid? How much of the past has been lost because someone was embarrassed to take notes?

You have to take that chance. This is the opportunity and the holy terror of making yourself ridiculous that every writer has to know to approach his own personal truth.

— THOMAS MCGUANE

244. The Armenian Story

Jessamyn West began to write when she was forty-three years old. She wrote twelve stories and sent each one to a different magazine, convinced they'd all be turned down. One magazine editor wrote back saying he liked her story very much, but he asked whether by any chance she was using a pseudonym. His magazine was for young Armenians. West was not going to let this brush with possible success escape, and she immediately went to her Napa Valley phone book to search for an Armenian name for herself. When she couldn't find one, she had to confess that no, she was not an Armenian, and so her story was not published. But for years every time that editor read one of her stories somewhere else, he would write to her, "Still sorry you're not a young Armenian."

You must be willing to stick your neck out, to take a chance, to risk making a fool of yourself and discovering you are a fool, if you want to write.

— JESSAMYN WEST

245. A Guy He Knew in High School

Once, on a long car trip with family, I discovered a slim hard-back novel in the backseat and asked about it. "Oh, it's by some guy I went to high school with," said my son-in-law. I started to read it, and read it all the way to our destination. The novel, just published, was *The Hours* by Michael Cunningham.

"So what was he like?" I kept asking, but I couldn't get any anecdotes or gossip out of my son-in-law. Apparently Michael Cunningham was just another classmate, a nice guy, at La Canada High School. After this I read an essay in which Cunningham wrote about becoming interested in Virginia Woolf to impress a girl he thought of as "the pirate queen of [his] high school." (I ask my son-in-law about this pirate queen in La Canada, and he has no idea what I'm talking about.) At age fifteen Cunningham didn't understand Woolf's *Mrs. Dalloway*, but he began to understand sentences and to fall in love with language when he tried to read it. Years later, when he knew that he was going to be a novelist, he wanted to write something about Virginia Woolf, but he kept putting it off, wanting to be smarter, more talented before he attempted it. Finally, in his early forties, he realized he'd never feel smart or talented enough, so he went ahead and wrote it anyway. *The Hours* was going to be the original title for Woolf's book until she changed it to *Mrs. Dalloway*. Cunningham won the Pulitzer Prize for his book.

Great art helps keep us mindful of the fact that the world is both local and universal, and that time is largely an illusion.

— MICHAEL CUNNINGHAM

246. Writer's Block

If you ask writers about writer's block, you'll get one of two reactions: Head nodding, total understanding — "Awful, awful," they'll murmur. Or a sniffy response that there's no such thing as writer's block, it's simply laziness, an indulgence, and all you need is a deadline.

Once I couldn't write — for a long time. I tried but came up with dreadful stuff. Little pinched paragraphs of fiction that had nowhere to go. But I kept writing them anyway, even though I felt like I was writing myself deeper into a hole.

A few years later I wrote the book I needed to read, and it felt like receiving the words by dictation.

If there were easy, rational answers to all of this, how simple writing would be.

To be a writer is to be a shuttlecock in a badminton game, one racquet of which is naïve optimism and the other a cynical despair.
— JOHN JEROME

247. The Perfect Book

In his preface to *Lights on a Ground of Darkness*, Pulitzer Prize winner and poet laureate Ted Kooser tells about how he dreamed of writing a book about his mother's family ever since he was a little boy. "This is a book I put off writing for more than fifty years because I wanted it to be perfect, which it is not and could never be," he says. "In almost every family there is someone like me who desperately wants to write such a story and is forever kept from it by fear of failure." Finally, when his mother was in her late eighties and dying, he sat down and wrote the memoir. Two months before her death he gave her a copy of the manuscript. He was afraid that it might make her sad, but he took the risk; to his relief she told him she liked what he had done.

Perfection is achieved, not when there is nothing more to add, but when there is nothing left to take away.

— Antoine de Saint-Exupéry

248. Ted Kooser Groupie

Okay, so I'm a big fan of Ted Kooser. One summer I'm teaching a nonfiction workshop at the same place he's guest poet at a poetry festival, and there he is teaching and reading his poems, wearing his jeans and cute shirts and looking very serious. He's the rock star of the poetry festival. Fans and students trail behind him wherever he goes, and my students and I sit in on his open lectures and readings. I'm not normally a shy person, but when I see him, I'm paralyzed with awe and awkwardness.

At the end of the festival, I buy two of his books and stand in line to have him autograph them. And then there he is, and he's holding his pen, and I hand him the books. "Barbara," I say. "My name is Barbara." He nods and opens the book to sign it. I want to say something to him so remarkable and cool that when he goes back to Nebraska and thinks about this week at Idyllwild, he might remember me. But I can't think of anything clever or cool. Instead, I say, "My mother was born in Lincoln." He nods again as he signs the book. And then I say, "You and I are the same age." He looks at me. "Well," he finally says. "We look pretty good, don't we?"

The best fame is a writer's fame: it's enough to get a table at a good restaurant, but not enough that you get interrupted when you eat.
— FRAN LEBOWITZ

249. Fabulous Mulch

Ray Bradbury said we all have three things in our head: (1) our experiences; (2) how we reacted and felt about those experiences; (3) the art experiences we've had through writers, artists, films, music, etc. He called all this "fabulous mulch."

When Bradbury began writing, he'd make noun lists — "the crickets," "the train whistle," "the basement" — and then he'd word-associate around each noun. He also made lists of things he hated and then lists of things he loved. "When I wrote *Fahrenheit 451* I hated book burners and I loved libraries," he said. "So there you are."

If you have the name for a thing or a creature you have control over it — in fantasy.

— JOYCE CAROL OATES

250. Fiction as Acting

Writing fiction can feel like doing a play or a movie. But you're not only the playwright or screenwriter; you're also the director, the costume designer, the location scout, the set designer, the prop master, and each and every actor.

This, of course, is the dangerous thing about fiction. You're finding those actors, those characters, inside yourself; they're part of you, and they're not always the part you care to show the world.

For me, acting is about discovering myself, discovering all the people who live in me....It's not about putting on a mask and costume and saying "I'm somebody else."

— LINDA LAVIN

251. Playing Sane

There's the real world, and then there's the world in your head when you're writing. There are the people driving to sensible jobs, putting gas in their cars, shopping for food, taking care of children. And then there are those of us who are delving into the deepest part of our souls at 11:00 AM or murdering someone on our computer at 3:00 in the afternoon.

After she writes all morning in a hotel room, Maya Angelou goes home and tries to act normal: "I go out and shop — I'm a serious cook — and pretend to be normal. I play sane — Good morning! Fine, thank you. And you?"

I've always felt that there's a very thin membrane between madness, alcoholism, and/or destitution and being an OK American guy in a comfortable heated apartment with meatballs and a decent Sauvignon Blanc in the fridge.

— AUGUST KLEINZAHLER

252. Looking out the Window Dreaming

I was never one of those kids out on the playground hanging by my heels from the monkey bars, acting fearless. And balls terrified me. Soccer, softball, dodgeball — I hated it all. Nor was I the kid in the front row making sense of math and diagramming sentences. I was the one looking out the window and daydreaming — fantasies of different lives, of being invisible, of being fearless.

I'm still doing that — and so is everyone who writes. Part of the job description is daydreaming.

Dreams are where other people escape from reality. But for the writer, dreams are the reality.

— ROGER ROSENBLATT

253. Attempting and Shaping

Essay comes from the French word *essai* — an "attempt" or "experiment." David Shields writes that in antiquity the Latin word for the essay was *experior*, "to try, test, experience, prove." He also says that the word *novel* once meant a formless form with no rules, or that one made up his or her own rules about it, and that the word *fiction* came from a word meaning to "shape, fashion, form or mold."

If the idea of your essay attempting or experimenting, or your novel shaping or molding, expands your imagination in any way, use it. Otherwise, simply ignore this etymology.

Every artistic movement from the beginning of time is an attempt to figure out a way to smuggle more of what the artist thinks is reality into the work of art.

— DAVID SHIELDS

254. What Your Headlights Reveal

One of the most famous of all writing quotes is from E. L. Doctorow: "Writing a novel is like driving a car at night. You can only see as far as your headlights but you can make the whole trip that way."

This has been quoted by dozens of other writers because the idea strikes a nerve with all of us who write. We all feel like we're writing in the dark, trying to get somewhere, and the idea that the road we have to travel will keep being revealed if we just keep driving is heartening.

Stop worrying where you're going. Move on.

— STEPHEN SONDHEIM

255. True to the Story

I once read about an actress who said the best advice she ever got from a director on opening night was, "Don't whore. Go out there and play the play."

This goes for writers too. Don't whore (unless you're marketing your book). Stay true to the story. Don't try to sell the reader something; don't try to impress. Make the writing invisible.

We can only be grateful that the work itself knocks self-consciousness out of the way, for it is only thus that the work can be done.

— MADELEINE L'ENGLE

256. Tasting the Spinach

Gordon Lish told his writing students: "As writers, you must try to keep yourselves alive, vibrant. Act as if you have never tasted the spinach. Be alert, be mindful."

Pay attention. Every day.

Be alert, be aware.

Taste the spinach.

Being a writer is a sanctuary, a haven in a heartless world.

— GORDON LISH

257. Fallow Periods

Larry McMurtry says it wasn't exactly writer's block that he suffered when his seventh book was almost finished; he still wrote his five pages every day, but he no longer liked his five pages. He suddenly hated his own prose. When he finished the book (*Terms of Endearment* — which he ended up liking), he went into a "literary gloom" that lasted eight years. And then he went on to write *Lonesome Dove* and a couple of dozen other novels.

Facing it — always facing it. That's the way to get through it. Face it.

— Joseph Conrad

258. Grace and Grit

"I write by grace and grit," wrote Terry Tempest Williams in "Why I Write."

These six words form about as perfect a sentence as I've ever read. The meaning of the sentence with the sound ("grace" *sounds* like grace, and "grit" *sounds* like grit) and the order of the words. Grace and grit. That's how we write.

I write knowing I will always fail. I write knowing words always fall short.

— TERRY TEMPEST WILLIAMS

259. Give Yourself Credit

How amazing to make up stories! You're creating a whole world out of your imagination — you're building all the furniture and the houses, making the roads, creating the weather, cooking the meals, sewing the clothes, not to mention giving birth to all your characters. This is hard work; no wonder writing is exhausting and can make us a little strange. Give yourself some credit for what you're doing.

Writing is almost always too hard, except when the story blows in.
— BETH KEPHART

260. The Mother Who Used the *F* Word

A student emails me all the less-than-glowing comments that her kids make about her essay. She does this no matter how many times I tell her not to show anything she writes to her family. I say this over and over to all my students — "Do not show your work to your family and/or close friends" — and no one ever pays any attention to me. Then I get anguished emails about boyfriends who are upset, children who dispute every other word written, threatening spouses, distraught mothers, etc.

When my kids were teenagers, I published my first novel, and the word *fuck* appeared in it maybe two times. My younger daughter, who was in junior high then, told me she was incredibly embarrassed that her friends might read this book and see that word. Now this child and her friends were far, far from being little prudes, but suddenly I was the Mother Who Used the *F* Word.

Maybe writers just can't be perfect parents, or possibly even very good parents, since they're always embarrassing their children. I adored this girl, still adore her, but I wasn't going to censor my language on the published page for her.

So one more time: do not let your kids, your family, read your stuff. But after it's published, they're on their own.

There is also one's inclination to be charming instead of presenting a grittier truth about the world. But then, having children has also made me this particular writer. Without my children, I'd have written with less fervor; I wouldn't understand life in the same way.
— LOUISE ERDRICH

261. If You Don't Write

What happens if you don't write? What if you just never wrote one more thing, imagined or otherwise? What if you let your days and dreams drift by without making notes? What if you just wrote the occasional email or text message and let it go at that?

There are no answers here — just the question to think about, maybe write about.

Getting to a place after many years where it seemed to me that if I didn't write, I would disappear. The diversions, because that's what they were, no longer diverted. I was left with myself and had to do the one thing I could to survive. I knew it would be difficult to write, very difficult, but I set about doing it.

— FREDERICK SEIDEL

262. Lish's Boots

"Own your first sentence, make it yours," said Gordon Lish. "If anybody can see your sentence better than you can see your sentence, you do not own it — they own it."

Lish was Raymond Carver's editor at Knopf, and he also taught writing in universities and in private classes. On the Internet I found thirty-five pages of notes one of his students took in his class: "Presentation, not representation." "You must come to the page without pettiness, without holding a grudge." I printed out the thirty-five pages, and now they're heavily underlined.

Another of Lish's students, Lily Tuck, wrote an essay about the class she took with him. "Writing," he said in the first class, "is a way of behaving and we must learn to behave importantly." She sat on the floor (it was a crowded class with not enough chairs) and studied his shoes — old-fashioned lace-up boots, highly polished, that looked custom-made.

"The writer has to seek to know the object and honor its unknowability when reporting on it," he said in the third class.

The more you feel the object you are rendering, the less you have to explain.

— GORDON LISH

263. Putting the Pieces Together

An agent once gave me the idea for a children's picture book. It was a brilliant idea — fresh (no other kids' books, to my knowledge, had tackled this), and it also hooked into some of my own memories. So I went right to work. The beginning went well — funny and true. I named a character Molly after the agent who had given me the idea. And then about half-way through the story, it all bogged down. I could not find an ending. But I couldn't let go of it, either. I'd pull it out of the file every couple of months and have another go at it, then get frustrated and put it away again. I'm not talking about the great American novel here but a picture book of about four hundred words. Yet I couldn't find those last words for *eight years*. When I tell my students about this, it tends to frighten them.

But sometimes writing is like a puzzle — and the pieces don't always arrive on schedule the way you think they should.

Life isn't a puzzle that needs to fit together perfectly, every piece locking into place with every other piece to form a perfect whole. Life is complicated. Stuff overlaps.

— ABIGAIL THOMAS

264. Writing on the Road

Take your work with you wherever you go. Little notebooks or cards for just leaving the house, bigger notebooks or your laptop for longer trips. You need to write on the road because if you leave your work behind, you can lose the rhythm. The very large space that your story takes up in your head gets filled with a dozen other things that have nothing to do with writing.

Jacqueline Winspear says she had no choice about starting to write on the road; she was on a long book tour and had a looming deadline for her next Maisie Dobbs novel, so in hotel rooms she'd just plug in her laptop and get on with it. Then it became apparent to her that her writing was doing what it always did — it was grounding her.

Between planes and taxis, the hotels and so many people met only once before I moved on again, my writing was a comfortable place of knowing I came back to every day. It was as if I was bringing my place of belonging with me, and it soothed me.

— JACQUELINE WINSPEAR

265. Good Luck

We need luck. But good luck only comes when we're working hard, not thinking about luck or success but driven by the passion we have for what we're doing. And if it's not the passion driving us, then the dark, crazed fear that we won't make it if we stop trying for an instant.

I feel about myself that I'm anomalous — a rare combination of fear, an affection for language, a reverence for literature, doggedness, and good luck.

— RICHARD FORD

266. Going for Magic

Dream big. And if you need to discuss your big dreams about your book with anyone, just make sure that he or she isn't the kind of person who will pop a nail into your balloon. It can sometimes take just one eye roll to finish off a really great idea for a book.

When I told Norma, my writing teacher, the idea for what was to become my first published novel (not to be confused with the many unpublished novels that came before it), she listened in an encouraging, attentive way and then said with absolute conviction, "I can see it in the bookstores." And I had the feeling she really could *see* it. So I had to write it.

You may dismiss this as la-la-land woo-woo — but whatever supplies the magic for you, believe in it.

What you can do, or dream you can, begin it; boldness has genius, power and magic in it.

— JOHANN WOLFGANG VON GOETHE

267. Writing in Trucks

Monica Holloway, who has published successful memoirs, including one about horrific events in her childhood, often comes to my class as a speaker. And she is so smart and articulate, open and funny, that she emboldens my students to write whatever it is that they've been afraid to write about. There's an element of rescue in her story for those who have lived through similar childhoods. She also talks about her fear of writing, how hard it can be, and she tells hilarious stories about writing in her truck but always finishing her books by checking into a Beverly Hills hotel and writing around the clock for a few days. My students love her and afterward talk to her as if she's a friend.

You never know when your poem will come to someone's rescue.

— MARGE PIERCY

268. The Artistic Coma

Dorothea Brande believed that the problems of the writer — being unable to start or starting and then getting stuck, writing only one wonderful thing, or only being able to write in a writing class — came from root personality problems: lack of confidence, self-respect, and freedom. She also believed that genius could be taught. She had very practical advice about inducing the "artistic coma" with a series of exercises, including writing pages early in the morning before doing anything else, and even gave the novice advice on typewriters, how much coffee you could drink, and how to take a walk. She wrote *Becoming a Writer* in 1934, and it reappeared in 1981 with an admiring foreword by John Gardner.

Her main message was this: "How good a piece of work emerges depends on you and your life: how sensitive, how discriminating you are, how closely your experience reflects the experience of your potential readers."

You are flexible and sturdy, like a good tool. You know what it feels like to work as an artist.

— DOROTHEA BRANDE

269. Hell and Other Material

I found out I had breast cancer on Valentine's Day 1997, exactly six months before my second wedding and right in the middle of planning for the wedding. It took a while, including months of treatment and a thumbs-up from my doctors, to think, *Wow, what great material.* After a year went by, I started a writing workshop at the Wellness Community for people who were dealing with cancer, and eventually I decided to write a book about the workshop — the wonderful stuff that these nonwriters were coming up with and the great prompts I had found in poems and stories of published writers who had gone through serious illnesses. I ended up writing and publishing the book, but to make it work I had to include my own story. My own great material. And so it became half memoir.

All the difficult stuff in life — it's your material, remember that. And if it doesn't kill you, you get to write about it.

The thing about going through hell is that you also have to fry eggs and pay bills and change into pajamas, so hell is usually set against the ordinary living room of your life. Here is ready-made perspective. Write it all down.

— ABIGAIL THOMAS

270. The Paradox of Rewriting

Here's the paradox: When you rewrite, you polish. You want to make your writing so good it almost disappears. But on the other hand, you don't want your writing to be too smooth, too wrung out. You want an edge to remain, veers and shifts, quirks. Some students get really anxious when I tell them this. They think I'm talking out of both sides of my mouth, and I am.

The process of rewriting is mostly a process of fighting through that thicket of sentences, cutting back to the one that says what's actually meant.

— JOHN JEROME

271. Writers as Flashers

The thing about being a writer, as my friend María Amparo Escandón says, is that we're acting like a subway flasher. This can be especially true for memoir and essay writers. Fiction writers can maintain a bit more dignity (but not a whole lot because now everybody knows what's lurking in their imaginations even if they maybe haven't actually experienced it). Sometimes when I read essays out loud at book events, I can't believe what's coming out of my mouth in front of perfect strangers. I have friends who are not writers, and most of them seem wonderfully dignified, much more mysterious and adult than I am.

Writing is...that oddest of anomalies: An intimate letter to a stranger.

— Pico Iyer

272. On the Ground

On the beach in the sand I see an empty jar of baby food. Questions rise up. It's cold out; who would take a small baby to the beach? There's a story right there for you, or maybe a new path in a story already begun. Odd details can lead you somewhere new and fresh. Check out what's at your feet; you never know where it can lead. See if it fits into your story, or starts you on a new one.

Writers write about things that other people don't pay much attention to.

— NATALIE GOLDBERG

273. Getting Published

Years ago a new student came to class and said that everyone had always told her she wrote wonderful letters and should write, so now was the time. She was in her late forties and nervous about putting herself to the test. A week or two into the course, she wrote an essay about something that had happened to her at the gym, and with hands shaking, she read it to the class. The essay was strange and weird and interesting — the class and I loved it. I told her to send it out immediately. She was stunned — *send it out?* Try to get it *published?* Yes, I said, and start with the big magazines first.

So she did. A few weeks later there was a hysterical but joyful message on my answering machine: she had just gotten word that a big magazine in New York wanted to publish her essay.

It is joyful to get published right away — but there's also a downside. She didn't get published again for a number of years, long enough to grow awful doubts about her own talent and to think that maybe the first essay was a fluke. Finally she had a story published in a good anthology, and I often think of her. That first essay wasn't a fluke. She had talent, and I hope she's still writing.

First publication is a pure, carnal leap into that dark which one dreams is life.

— HORTENSE CALISHER

274. Sharks

Joy Williams thinks writing is absurd work; writers turn away from real days and nights to come up with other days and nights made out of words. "Oh, it's silly, dangerous work indeed," she writes. She also believes that the disorienting truth of being a writer is that the significant story has more awareness than the writer writing it. We the readers just want the story, and we don't care how the writer does it or why.

I'm dazzled by her essay on this subject. I love her take-no-prisoners attitude, her total lack of sentimentality, her cranky dismissal of writing as comfort, backed up by her story of being unable to help her mother when she was dying. I love that she admires Don DeLillo and thinks he's like a shark moving hidden in our midst. I love her fiction.

But I don't agree that we don't want to know why a writer does it and how.

Why do I write? Because I wanna be a great shark too. Another shark. A different shark, in a different part of the ocean. The ocean is vast.

— Joy Williams

275. Further Dazzle

On the other hand, the joy Carolyn See can find in writing is equally dazzling.

"If you can stand the dailiness of it — the continuing marriage of your inner life to all the confusion of the outside world — you can have some *fun!* — in the very highest and most profound sense." This is from her book *Making a Literary Life*, written for people who want to make a literary life for themselves, including, she writes, "folks who live in parts of the country where the idea of writing is about as strange as crossbreeding a tomato and trout." (I have to admit that I've been jealous of that sentence ever since I first read it.)

Why write? Carolyn See says: "Because we live in a beautiful, sentient universe that yearns for you to tell the truth about it. If you love this world and this craft, they will lift you to a place you can't begin to imagine."

The writing life is a life lived with all the windows and doors opened.... And rendering what one sees through those opened windows and doors in language is a way of bearing witness to the mystery of what it is to be alive in this world.

— JULIA ALVAREZ

276. God's Own Little Acre

Jim Harrison writes about how we writers are small gods with forty acres in which to reinvent the world. You can cultivate this acreage, but there's always going to be a bigger world beyond our grasp.

Anne Lamott writes about everybody getting their own emotional acre, including the characters in our stories. In specific ways they either take care of their acre or not. What does your character's acre look like? What is he or she growing? This may or may not show up in your writing, she says, but it's a way of finding out more about his or her inner life.

Think about your own land, one acre or forty. It's your chance at creating your own utopia. You might even write about it.

A work of art is a corner of creation seen through a temperament.
— Émile Zola

277. Paddling in a Bathtub

To abandon an unpublished novel is like jettisoning a whole world — mountains and trees, people and houses. An earthquake of destruction. And it happens at some time or another to just about everyone who writes novels.

Michael Chabon killed the novel he had started after the success of his first novel. "[It was] erasing me, breaking me down, burying me alive, drowning me, kicking me down the stairs," he said about the second novel's effect on him as he wrote. He had worked five and a half years on it.

Harper Lee, after the success of *To Kill a Mockingbird*, gave up on the one hundred pages of a new novel she'd tried to write. She told a cousin, "When you're at the top there's only one way to go."

One of the livelier stories of a writer abandoning his work is when Evelyn Waugh burned his first unpublished novel in 1925 after a friend read it and didn't like it. He then tried to drown himself, only to be stung by jellyfish. He returned to shore and eventually started another novel.

Look, writing a novel is like paddling from Boston to London in a bathtub. Sometimes the damn tub sinks. It's a wonder that most of them don't.

— STEPHEN KING

278. Where It All Starts

There are a lot of movie shoots in my neighborhood. The parking lot next door to my house will fill up with trailers for actors, costume trailers, catering trucks, tents and tables, tons of cameras and lights and other equipment, cars, and dozens of people. It's like a little instant city.

And you know where it all started? With one person alone in a room writing down one word, and then another word and another.

Writing is the underpinning, infrastructure, point of departure, reason and pretext for all of it.

— DIANE KEATON

279. Descriptions of Palos Verdes

My first published novel involved a graphic rape and a murder committed by the victim of the rape. The setting was Palos Verdes, California, where I was living at the time. My father read my book sitting on the couch in my living room during a visit, and I tiptoed around him for two days as he read, feeling queasy about his reading all the graphic violence I'd written.

"Well!" he said when he finished it. "That was certainly interesting. I really enjoyed the descriptions of Palos Verdes."

Writers will happen in the best of families. No one is quite sure why.
— RITA MAE BROWN

280. The Jewels

A student reads a line that is so evocative that everyone in class comments on it. She emails me later that she's going to save it for another story, a better story. "No!" I email back. "Use it now!" Annie Dillard says, "The impulse to save something good for a better place later is the signal to spend it now. Something more will arise for later, something better."

It's hard to believe when you hit on a perfect line or paragraph or description that more will come. You want to place this amazing piece of writing like a little jewel in the best possible setting.

Don't let it become too precious; spend it, use it. Joan Didion once said that she used the good silver every day because today is all we have.

Anything you do not give freely and abundantly becomes lost to you. You open your safe and find ashes.

— Annie Dillard

281. Antidote for Age Angst

Maybe you're sitting around right now feeling old. Too old to begin a writing career, or too old to try a second book or a tenth, or too old to start writing an essay or a poem — you feel over the hill. Maybe you've lost heart for this whole enterprise.

Here's a story to help you snap out of your age angst. Toyo Shibata started writing poetry at age ninety-two (up until then she had danced traditional Japanese dances as a hobby, but her back gave out). She sent one of her poems to a newspaper, and they published it; so she sent them another one. Eventually, when she was ninety-nine, she self-published a collection of her poems. Her book, *Don't Be Too Frustrated*, became a surprise bestseller in Japan, and right now 1.5 million copies are in print. Her second book will be published on her one hundredth birthday.

I think of various things: memories of my past and my family, my current life. I immerse myself in those memories and write from them.

— Toyo Shibata

282. Another Tale of Inspiration

Harriet Doerr went back to college after her husband died, and she was sixty-seven years old when she finally graduated from Stanford. Around that time she began writing stories and sent them out to small magazines. The stories then evolved into her first novel. After a lot of rejections, *Stones for Ibarra* was published by Viking in 1984 and won the National Book Award.

I'm quite happy working on a sentence for an hour or more, search-ing for the right phrase, the right word. I compare it to the work of a stone cutter, chipping away at the raw material until it's just right, or as right as you can get it.

— HARRIET DOERR

283. A Mess of Questions and Detail

At sunrise Nelson and I are out on the beach, and an older guy in black shorts and a gray T-shirt runs by in the opposite direction with an attractive young woman. I hear him say to her, "Esalen? Michael Murphy?" I strain for more, but they've already passed me. About fifteen minutes later I hear two men behind me talking, and one says, "Don't worry, you should be able to get a ticket. Welcome to LA!" It's the same older guy in the black shorts and gray shirt — who then runs past me, alone now, in the other direction.

How did he start talking to the young woman, and why, about Esalen and Michael Murphy? And in fifteen minutes how did he start a whole new conversation with a stranger? A ticket to what? When I glance back at the stranger he had been talking to, I notice he's wearing black pants and a gray shirt too. I'm wearing gray pants and a black shirt.

Nonwriters would think it's crazy to stand out there on the beach at 6:10 in the morning, writing down overheard dialogue and noting what we're all wearing and that the clouds today look like little quotation marks in the sky. And maybe it is crazy. But it's what writers do.

As a writer, I don't have ideas for books. I have little bits and pieces of life, little spoken lines and little gestures and settings all represented in language which I then put into a sequence and make into a kind of logic.

— RICHARD FORD

284. Keeping Faith

What is faith? "Belief not based on proof," says my dictionary. "Confidence and belief in something outside of yourself."

For Gail Godwin keeping faith means staying in her study no matter how much she wants to leave. She says sometimes it means going to work "*without hope* and *without energy* and simply acknowledging my own barrenness and lighting my incense and turning on my computer."

Faith in your own writing will always have its ups and downs, but faith in the act of writing, faith in literature as a saving grace, faith in the written word to forge connection and make change — this is what we keep, love, and never let go of.

When I am working, I move into an area of faith which is beyond the conscious control of my intellect. . . . The challenge is to let my intellect work for *the creative act, not against it.*

— MADELEINE L'ENGLE

285. Writers' Words

In *The Novelist's Lexicon* writers from all over the world were asked to choose one word that defines their fiction. Rick Moody chose *adumbrated*, meaning produced as a faint image or resemblance, outlined or sketched, foreshadowed. Alissa York chose *creature*: "The novel is a creature. As such, it begins with the greatest of mysteries in the smallest of ways." Jonathan Lethem — *furniture*: "However appalling to consider, however tedious to enact, every novel requires furniture, whether it is to be named or unnamed, for the characters will be unable to remain in standing positions for the duration of the story." Peter Stamm chose *honesty*; Ludmila Ulitskaya — *insomnia*; Tariq Ali — *laughter*; Ying Chen — *phantom*. Anne Weber turned two words into her word: *waiting/attention*: "Writing, more than anything, is a matter of not writing. And of attentive waiting."

Watch out for words that strike a pose.

— NICOLAS FARGUES

286. The Four Stages of Receiving Feedback

When you get really serious and tough comments on your work, there are various stages you go through. The first stage for me is usually a panic attack. This can be followed almost immediately by the second stage: *What do they know?* And/or: *They're right — it's all crap!* (Since I've been writing and getting feedback for a long time, I zip through these stages pretty fast.)

If the feedback is coming from someone you respect (and hopefully not related to you by blood or past history), and if this person has read your work seriously and pondered how you can make it deeper and better, then the third stage will be the dawning of gratitude: how wonderful to find someone who is honest and tough but also points out the worth of what you're writing! The fourth stage is inspiration. An honest critique can actually inspire you to forge on.

Feedback that isn't solely about the absolute perfection of your writing is simply part of getting published. Even if you sell a novel or memoir, be prepared for many notes and, if you're lucky, *pages* of feedback from your editor.

It's hard for us to open ourselves to rebuff.... If you're going to write and be published, you've got to expect to have a few arrows thrown at you.

— MADELEINE L'ENGLE

287. How the Light Gets In

What illuminates? What shines? What kind of writing — or acting or dance or music or painting — moves us and shakes up our life? Because that's what it's all about, isn't it? Illuminating life, loving the shine of the world, and also the cracks, shaking things up. It's about truth, not perfection.

Forget your perfect offering
There is a crack, a crack in everything
That's how the light gets in.

— LEONARD COHEN

288. What Is It About?

Vivian Gornick believes that you cannot teach people how to express themselves in a dramatic way or how to find structure for a memoir, but that you can teach them how to read and how to judge a piece of writing. Which, of course, translates into judging their own writing as well and, the hope is, making it more expressive and finding structure for it.

"What is this all about?" she asks, holding up a memoir manuscript a student is working on. The student replies, "It's about this family." Gornick says, "No, no. What is it *about*?"

What is it that makes a piece of writing larger than its immediate story? What is the inner purpose, what connects this story to something larger than the family being written about? What is the compelling reason for people to read this memoir? Why are you writing it?

These are the questions we have to ask ourselves over and over as we write.

Writing enters into us when it gives us information about ourselves that we are in need of at the time we are reading.

— VIVIAN GORNICK

289. Simplicity

No one can say it better than Chekhov: "Cross out as many adjectives and adverbs as you can. You have so many modifiers that the reader has trouble understanding and gets worn out. It is comprehensible when I write: 'The man sat on the grass,' because it is clear and does not detain one's attention. On the other hand, it is difficult to figure out and hard on the brain if I write: 'The tall, narrow-chested man of medium height and with a red beard sat down on the green grass that had already been trampled down by the pedestrians, sat down silently, looking around timidly and fearfully.' The brain can't grasp all that at once, and art must be grasped at once, instantaneously."

Omit needless words.

— WILLIAM STRUNK, JR.

290. Clean as a Bone

James Baldwin said rewriting was painful to him and he had to do a lot of it. Most of his rewriting was "cleaning" — not describing but showing. The hardest thing for him was simplicity. "And the most fearful thing, too," he said. "You have to strip yourself of all your disguises, some of which you didn't know you had. You want to write a sentence as clean as a bone."

Raymond Carver loved rewriting — and would do up to twenty or thirty drafts of a story. In the final version of those stories, the "writing" is invisible, clean as a bone.

I write one page of masterpiece to ninety-one pages of shit. I try to put the shit in the wastebasket.

— ERNEST HEMINGWAY

291. What Editors Look For

I teach an advanced class in nonfiction that students have to submit work to get into. Since the class is limited to twelve students, I spend a lot of time going over their submissions; it feels like being an editor deciding whose work to publish. First of all, I throw out any manuscript that's sloppy or hard to read (which is what any editor or agent would do). Then I simply look for a story I want to hear more of, one that makes me want to find out what happens next, and that's written in clear, simple language. And this is what every editor and agent you send your work to is looking for.

Approach agents and editors with care.

— NOAH LUKEMAN

292. Pressure

You're now deep into your year of writing dangerously/ wildly/passionately, or maybe it's more like a year of writing slowly and painfully — or perhaps all of the above. You have another few months if you want to have a first draft of a book completed, or some stories or essays finished. It's good to put pressure on yourself. Give yourself this deadline, this pressure to finish. No one else will until you sell a book or a short piece and acquire an editor. Then it's both a joy and a sword hanging over your head to have deadlines coming from the outside.

I had a yoga teacher once who said it's important that if you fall out of a balance pose you go right back into it. This is like your own deadline; if you don't make it, give yourself another one right away.

If I ever got something in on time, which would mean I'd let it go from this house and liked it...well, that's never happened in my life....I've never sent a piece of anything that's finished.... There's not even a proper ending to Fear and Loathing in Las Vegas. *I had several different endings in mind, another chapter or two, one of which involved going to buy a Doberman.*

— HUNTER S. THOMPSON

293. Pruning Pages

None of us really wants to hear how incredibly easy and magical it feels to write a novel; writing a novel is more like a daily battle between optimism and plummeting self-esteem. It's hard and it's long. That's why Annie Dillard was so inspiring in a radio interview when she said that her latest book had taken her *ten years* to write and she had to cut it from 1,200 pages to 230. She sounded put out and cranky about the whole thing and vowed she'd never write another novel. You have to simplify the story, she said, and then expand it. She went through every single word in the final draft, cut out as many modifiers as possible, tried to find one- or two-syllable words instead of words with three or more, and made sure there were no passive verbs. (This is about as good a piece of advice about revising as you'll ever come across.)

She said that Books on Tape had wanted to edit a previous book of hers from eight tapes down to two. She fought it but finally agreed to four tapes. When they sent her the pruned manuscript, she was thrilled; she thought the book was so much better with their cuts.

I cut adjectives, adverbs, and every word which is there just to make an effect. Every sentence which is there just for the sentence.
— GEORGES SIMENON

294. The Edge of a Long Silence

When Richard Rodriguez was about to start writing an autobiography, a New York editor told him that it would be a lonely journey. "There will be times when you will think the entire world has forgotten you," he said to Rodriguez.

But that loneliness never made Rodriguez forget that this work was also public. "Write about something else in the future," his mother had written to him seven years before in a letter when he published his first personal essay. "Our family life is private," she said. "Why do you need to tell the *gringos* about how 'divided' you feel from your family?"

Some people have told me how wonderful it is that I am the first in my family to write a book. I stand on the edge of a long silence.
— RICHARD RODRIGUEZ

295. The Prize

What are you after?

As Kevin Spacey told a group of young actors when they asked how you get through the lean years to the prize, "There is no prize."

Of course, selling your work might feel like a prize — for about fifteen minutes. Or sometimes maybe a whole week if it's a book. But then comes the reality of edits and going over the page proofs word by word, thinking it's certainly not as wonderful as it was before you started writing the damn thing. Then comes marketing: the book is published finally, and you turn into a salesperson. Actually I think of myself at this point as the Marketing Whore. It's like having five thousand heads of lettuce in the warehouse that you have to move out and sell as soon as you can, *in any way possible*.

If there is a prize in all this, it's the writing. No matter how hard it can be sometimes, how scary, that's the best part — we get to do the thing we love.

In the end it's about enriching the lives of those who will read your work and enriching your own life as well. It's about getting up, getting well, getting over, getting happy, okay? Getting happy.
— STEPHEN KING

296. Expectations

Though maybe on some level we all write to have someone recognize us — to say, "Oh, that's who you really are" — and to finally know us, understand us, and respect and love us, it's best to keep our expectations low.

Staceyann Chin says that when she put together the broken pieces of her life and made a story out of them, she thought that her family would applaud her. But she says, "Instead they are ashamed of me for being so loud, so lesbian, even if they are secretly proud of me for being on *The Oprah Winfrey Show*, and being able to pay my own rent, or theirs sometimes.... They believe something is really wrong with me for telling so much to so many."

In the end it's like wanting to be loved for the way we lay bricks or teach a class or build bridges or conduct a symphony or clean a house. It may happen, but the people you live with or see every day will probably not be impressed.

Bless you, my daughter. I know how much your writing matters. *The sweetness of both those statements, so rarely put together! Daughter and writer. Part of la familia and also my own person, that full and impossible combination! Isn't that what we all want — to put it all together and become that bigger version of our selves and still be loved by those who have only partially known us?*

— JULIA ALVAREZ

297. Enter Lusting

Years ago in New York I had a songwriter boyfriend who suggested that we write a dirty novel. We were both out of work and in need of money. Apparently there was a huge market for such novels, so I thought why not? This was so many years ago that the "dirty novel" couldn't use real words for body parts, nor the *f* word, but you did have to pop your characters into bed every other minute.

We set ourselves a three-week deadline and made long lists of suggestive verbs: — *grind*, *pump*, *press*, *writhe*, etc. — and then adverbs and adjectives, trying to come up with ordinary words that sounded innocent but in context weren't. Every day for three weeks we sat in my apartment on East Ninetieth Street shouting out new words for our lists and batting back and forth our so-called plot. God knows what the neighbors thought.

Unlike my later attempt at romance novels, this one was successful, and we sold it for a decent price. It was the first time I made money from writing. As a joke, we titled it *Enter Lusting*. Our editor topped that by publishing it as *Have Heels Will Travel*.

I have never been a title man. I don't give a damn what it is called.
— JOHN STEINBECK

298. The View in Your Head

Though Nadine Gordimer's writing room looks out on what she describes as a jungle — "a green darkness of tree ferns, calla lilies…four frangipani trees with delicate gray limbs" — her desk faces a blank wall, and the real view is inside her head. "For the hours that I'm at work," she writes, "I'm physically in my home in Johannesburg. But in the combination of awareness and senses that every fiction writer knows, I am in whatever elsewhere the story is in."

Some writers pin up maps and photographs or drawings of their characters' surroundings, and literally create another view. "We don't need a view; we are totally engaged in those views created by and surrounding the people we are getting to know," says Gordimer.

All I need is a window not to write.

— Tobias Wolff

299. Why Writers Get Stumped

When an interviewer asked Hemingway how much rewriting he did, Hemingway replied that it depended but that he had to rewrite the last page of *A Farewell to Arms* thirty-nine times.

"Was there some technical problem?" asked the interviewer. "What was it that had stumped you?"

"Getting the words right," said Hemingway.

No matter how much I rewrite, I never reach the destination. Even after decades of writing, the same still holds true.

— HARUKI MURAKAMI

300. The World's Worst Sentence

The worst sentence I ever read appeared in a fancy, one might say ostentatious, catalog from an upscale shopping plaza (that shall remain nameless): "[Nameless upscale shopping plaza] reflects a substance of rare statehood with its distinguished eminence."

This sentence, in a catalog that was mailed to a couple of million people, is totally meaningless (*statehood?*). And what on earth is *distinguished eminence* when it comes to a shopping mall? It's just bloated, pretentious language.

All that's required with our writing is that we don't confuse the reader and that we say something true in clear and simple language. And may we never use the words *distinguished* and *eminence* in the same sentence. Or perhaps ever.

Avoid fancy words.

— E. B. WHITE

301. Aha Moments

Over half a century and forty books ago, when Beverly Cleary was a children's librarian in Yakima, Washington, a little boy asked her, "Where are the books about kids like us?" This was her aha moment. She could only find one book for the boy about farm kids — so she began to write one herself.

Finding the idea for a book can be like a huge gift from the universe, but you have to be waiting, listening, watching for it. More than likely you'll write the book you need to read, and that someone else needs to read too.

I usually get the title for a book first, and I type it up immediately. I sit there and look at it and admire it, and I think to myself, I just need 4,000 sentences to go with this and I'll have a book.

— BETSY BYARS

302. A Reason to Read Newspapers

In 1982 Allan Gurganus read an article in the *New York Times* about a few widows of Confederate soldiers who were still alive and receiving government pensions. In the article was the phrase "oldest living Confederate widow." To say that he was wildly inspired by this phrase is an understatement. He sat down, wrote for four hours, and came up with the first thirty pages of his novel *Oldest Living Confederate Widow Tells All*.

I like to write stuff that's only an inch from life, from what really happened, but all the art is of course in that inch.

— GEOFF DYER

303. Papering Bathrooms

Your writing will get rejected. You will receive generic rejection slips, and if you're lucky, you'll receive some personal rejection notes. You will wallpaper your bathroom with these slips and notes. Or you will keep them in a big basket on your desk to fuel your resolve to get published.

You will feel like the little engine that could.

And you can.

Beyond talent lie all the usual words: discipline, love, luck, but, most of all, endurance.

— JAMES BALDWIN

304. Driven to Fiction

We're driven to write fiction for so many different reasons — because we love to make up stories and live different lives, because we want to translate real life into art and make sense of our lives, because we want to write what really happened but not make anybody mad at us. (You might want to rethink this last reason.)

Jim Crace talks about the conventional idea that novels are driven by our own experience. That we dig into our own past to write our fiction. However, he has a very happy, settled life, so he says his fiction is truly fiction. But for those writers who are writing about their own lives, he says: "Well, of course they're *driven*. When they leave the office…they take their subject matter with them. When they talk to their spouse, when they walk the dog, their subject matter is still sitting on their shoulder because they *are* their own subject matter."

I can't raid my past for raw material because my past is so dull, so I have to make it all up, I have to start from scratch, inventing alternate landscapes to fill with invented people and invented narratives.

— JIM CRACE

305. A Poem's Journey

Philip Levine thought if he could translate his experience of working in Detroit automobile factories into poems, he could "give it the value and dignity it did not begin to possess on its own." If he could write about it, he could come to understand it, but while working in the factories, he could find nothing poetic about the experience.

In the beginning he was too angry, he felt too exploited along with his coworkers, to write about factory work. "It's the imagination," he says, "that gives us poetry.... You have to follow where the poem leads. And it will surprise you. It will say things you didn't expect to say. And you look at the poem and you realize, 'That is truly what I felt. That is truly what I saw.'"

Later he won the Pulitzer Prize and became poet laureate for translating his blue-collar life into poetry.

I'm like the first person to go on this little journey. Whether the poem is going to find some branch to land on is a driving curiosity. Some poems don't go anywhere, and I just get rid of them.

— BILLY COLLINS

306. Rescue Operation

Stories can rescue people, and writers can also rescue stories.

Kate Atkinson says she feels like a voyeur at times because if someone who's not a writer tells her something interesting, she always asks if she can use it so that it's not a waste of an experience. "It is always a shame when there are these terrific things that don't get recorded, don't get written about, because that person is not a writer. In a way, you are rescuing experiences constantly — other people's experiences, your own experiences, the imaginative experience — it is a rescue operation."

Stories are precious. The idea of rescuing them is perhaps more accurate than stealing them.

Two or three things I know for sure and one of them is that telling the story all the way through is an act of love.

— Dorothy Allison

307. Typewriters vs. Computers

When my first husband gave me a blue electric typewriter, I was less than gracious about the gift. I hated the noise it made, as if it were waiting impatiently, *humming*, while I tried to come up with something to write. My old manual typewriter had worked just fine. But then I got used to the blue one, and when my second husband (before he was my husband) started calling me a Luddite and saying that all writers had to have a computer, I dug my heels in about computers too. And then he gave me a computer.

I like tools to be invisible; I don't want to think about learning something new while I'm struggling to write. But of course now you'd have to pry my computer from my cold, dead hands to take it away.

Julian Barnes is not fond of computers for his writing. He says, "They tend to make things look finished sooner than they are. I believe in a certain amount of physical labor; novel-writing should feel like a version — however distant — of traditional work."

On the other hand, Ian McEwan says, "Word processing is more intimate, more like thinking itself. In retrospect, the typewriter seems a gross mechanical obstruction. I like the provisional nature of unprinted material held in the computer's memory — like an unspoken thought."

I agree with both of them.

I write on paper with a dipped pen and ink, and type on a manual typewriter in order to have some three-dimensional activities with my hands — but again and again I discover how far words are capable of going, both in the world and on the page.

— Susan Minot

308. Baring Your Soul

Anne Sexton once said, "Be specific. Tell almost the whole story. Put your ear close down to your soul and listen hard."

Almost is a key word here. What to tell of the truth — in poetry, in memoir, in essay, in fiction? How much of your soul to bare? One of the elements we love in good stories is mystery, revealing experience and character, layer by layer.

We're trying to shape the truth — into art, into story, into a deeper, more universal truth. Listen hard, and tell almost the whole story.

Tell all the Truth but tell it slant.

— EMILY DICKINSON

309. Sailing from Context

You might think that you need more experiences, more far-ranging adventure in your life, to be a writer. But sometimes experience and adventure can backfire on you.

I sailed to Greece from Los Angeles with my first husband in a forty-four-foot boat we had just bought that neither of us was too clear on how to sail. To say we had a few adventures is like saying Joyce Carol Oates has written a few stories. What we assumed to be pirates circled our boat for hours off the coast of Central America and then, thankfully, disappeared. We lost the engine during a storm at the entrance of the Panama Canal and nearly crashed on the rocks. In the Caribbean, the U.S. Coast Guard, thinking we were drug runners, sprang a surprise visit to us under sail in the middle of the night to search the boat (causing us to think *they* were drug runners). En route from Greece to Yugoslavia we sailed too close to Albania, and the Albanian navy, such as it was, held us at gunpoint for a few hours before letting us head on to Dubrovnik. One might think this is amazing material, and it is, of course, but other than three chapters of a very bad failed novel, I have never written about it. (Probably because I was having this tiny nervous breakdown for most of the trip.)

Sometimes you're so overwhelmed that you can't write. All you can do is take notes. And that's what I did. Dozens of journals, pages and pages of notes. Finding the context was my problem. What did all this mean? And to this day I'm not sure. It was simply, and not so simply, a lot of experience.

What happened to the writer is not what matters; what matters is the large sense the writer is able to make of what happened.
— VIVIAN GORNICK

310. Nose to the Grindstone

When Woody Allen was asked what he had learned during all the years of writing and making movies, he said he hadn't learned much except to ignore the "peripheral nonsense" and to keep his nose to the grindstone; to just do the work and not read reviews.

I don't want to achieve immortality through my work; I want to achieve it through not dying.

— WOODY ALLEN

311. Committing Acts of Literature

Billy Collins says, "I have no work habits whatsoever.... The poem will come along when it arrives. I don't write every day. I try to be on the lookout for creative opportunities, something that might trigger a poem, but I don't sit down in the morning and try to commit an act of literature before lunch."

Annie Proulx doesn't have a routine, either. "I struggle to find time to write," she says. "Yesterday I had a lot of writing to do and I couldn't do it because a neighboring ranch called to say they were going to put bulls out in the pasture there. So I had to...stop the bulls from coming through onto my property. And that's what happened to the afternoon. So I don't have a set schedule for writing."

On the other hand, Ted Kooser writes from 4:30 to 7:30 every morning. Jonathan Franzen starts writing at 7:00 every morning and works six or seven days a week. And Flannery O'Connor once wrote to a friend: "I'm a full-time believer in writing habits, pedestrian as it all may sound. You may be able to do without them if you have genius but most of us only have talent and this is simply something that has to be assisted all the time by physical and mental habits or it dries up and blows away."

Turn up for work. Discipline allows creative freedom. No discipline equals no freedom.

— JEANETTE WINTERSON

312. Uncertainty

We don't usually know where our story is going — even when it's memoir (what memories will appear, where we will really end up, what it will mean) — and this always feels dangerous and risky to me.

Courage isn't about bravado and strength of character. It's about leaving a safe place to do something difficult in spite of the fear, and not knowing the results.

Making art is chancy — it doesn't mix well with predictability. Uncertainty is the essential, inevitable and all-pervasive companion to your desire to make art. And tolerance for uncertainty is the prerequisite to succeeding.
— DAVID BAYLES and TED ORLAND, Art & Fear

313. Mantra

Nikki Giovanni wrote a poem for writers about how we seek
and hide, break and mend, "We teach and learn / We write."
One of the ways we teach and learn is by writing the book we
need to read.

*You climb a long ladder until you can see over the roof, or over the
clouds. You are writing a book.*

— ANNIE DILLARD

314. Hype

There was an ad for self-publishing in a writing magazine that said: "Write Anything! Publish Everything! Market Everywhere!" I wanted to shout back: "No, no! Do not write *anything*! Do not publish *everything*! And where oh where is this *everywhere*?"

The ad ended with: "Visit our website. It's that simple."

You know and I know it isn't that simple.

But we writers are vulnerable, so beware of hype. Hopefully we write *everything* only in our first drafts, and only publish our very best writing, and only after someone we trust edits it. And unless you're a bestselling author, you do our own marketing.

There's no easy route to publishing, even with self-publishing. But it's possible. And self-publishing can be enormously satisfying — either as autobiographies for your family or books about your work that you have a built-in network to sell to. It's hard work, but engaging and interesting and exciting. Just not simple and easy.

There are men that will make you books and turn 'em loose into the world with as much dispatch as they would do a dish of fritters.
— MIGUEL DE CERVANTES

315. Flying off Course

Marc Allen uses an airplane analogy when he talks about staying on track with a positive attitude to reach success: 95 percent of the time that a plane is in the air, it's off course, so the pilot has to keep making corrections in order to reach the destination.

Writers can get off course a lot. Not only when we're writing but also when we listen to that critic carping in our head, when going to our desk feels risky, or when we're smacked in the face by a rejection.

The Japanese idea of *kaizen* is helpful — making one small change every day to reach a goal, one small correction every day or hour or minute to reach your destination.

What lies behind us and lies before us are small matters compared to what lies within us.

— RALPH WALDO EMERSON

316. The Bottom Line

Someone once yelled out to an elderly Robert Frost, "Congratulations on your longevity!"

Frost called back, "To hell with my longevity, read my books!"

Maybe it's because I'm a writer, but it always seems like the decent thing is to buy *a book.*

— AMY HEMPEL

317. Pages Like Dresden

A perfect first draft is like someone sitting down at a piano for the first time and playing a perfect Beethoven sonata. Except that everyone can understand that it takes years and years of practice before playing the sonata. But since we know how to write anyway — well, why do we have to practice so much?

Roger Rosenblatt tells his students that they should be able to see the wreckage of their early drafts — the crossed-out words, phrases, sentences. "Slash and burn! Bombs away! Our pages should look like Dresden."

The difference between the almost right word and the right word is really a large matter — 'tis the difference between the lightning bug and the lightning.

— MARK TWAIN

318. Making Useful Tables and Chairs

I think there are two kinds of writers — carpenters and sculptors. Most of us are carpenters. We saw and hammer words, nail sentences together, sand and polish, trying to create something useful. Like a kitchen table, maybe, or a sturdy chair.

But then there are the sculptors. Writers and poets who simply take our breath away with how they can mold life into art with words. These are the writers and poets who inspired us to write in the first place.

We need to read the sculptors for inspiration and to think of our own writing as a useful craft that we just keep practicing.

[He] had a draper's touch for the unfolding fabric of a sentence, and he collected words like rare buttons.

— DIANE ACKERMAN

319. Quick!

In the opening line of her poem "Exact," Rae Armantrout asks for the exact shade of a hotel carpet, and the next line is: "Quick, before you die."

Quick. First thought, best thought?

We have to ask ourselves over and over, quick, a word for the way that branch moves in the wind, the way someone you love picks up a cup of coffee, the sound of a freeway. Quick. Don't be lazy — look for the exact move, the precise color, the specific sound that no one has ever put into words before.

I'd have to be really quick
to describe clouds.

— WISLAWA SZYMBORSKA

320. Reading Where Written

It is strange, yet wonderful and illuminating, to read a book in the place where it was written. There are layers: the book itself, the impact of place, plus your own experience in this place. Reading *Gift from the Sea* on Captiva, the island off the coast of Florida where Anne Morrow Lindbergh wrote the book, reading the edition that includes her daughter's foreword written fifty years later, and being on the island collecting seashells with your own daughter and granddaughter while remembering the first time you read this book years ago — creates a swirl of memory and feeling.

You realize too the lasting power of a generous and thoughtful book.

I began these pages for myself, in order to think out my own particular pattern of living, my own individual balance of life, work and human relationships. And since I think best with a pencil in my hand, I started naturally to write.

— ANNE MORROW LINDBERGH

321. To Have and to Have Not

When Mary Oliver was very young and knew that she wanted to be a poet, she made a list of all the things she'd never have. A house of her own, a new car, great clothes, and good restaurants. She knew poets never made any money. She took some teaching jobs over the years but none that she thought would be interesting; she wanted to save her energy for her writing.

The irony, of course, is that she not only won a Pulitzer Prize but also became one of the rock stars of poetry, able to fill large auditoriums with devoted, applauding fans. This most ardent lover of nature and simplicity ended up with the ability to acquire great material comfort if she so desired.

What are you willing to give up to write? But what is the cost if you don't write?

Money in our culture is equal to power. And money, finally, means very little because power, in the end, means nothing.
— MARY OLIVER

322. Eighty Percent of Success

We don't have to know what we're going to write in order to write. It's so simple — why can't we remember that?

Didn't Woody Allen say that just showing up is 80 percent of success?

Success usually comes to those who are too busy to be looking for it.
— HENRY DAVID THOREAU

323. Back Up!

Dorothy Allison writes about standing on a street in Los Angeles looking at a friend's car that had just been robbed. "You have a copy, right?" asked her friend.

Allison's manuscript notebook for *Bastard out of Carolina* had been stolen, and sixty pages in it existed nowhere else.

My friend Deb had three years of writing disappear when her computer was stolen from her car.

Here's what could possibly be the most valuable advice in this book (and I speak from experience): You must back up your work on the computer and make copies. You must also click Save as you write.

All that remains of my complete works are three pencil drafts of a bum poem which was later scrapped, some correspondence between John McClure and me, and some journalistic carbons.

— ERNEST HEMINGWAY

324. Paranoia and Manuscripts

I'm so paranoid I worry that the little black box attached to my computer backing up every word I type might not survive the next LA earthquake. So periodically I email an attachment of my current manuscript to family who live out of state. Without commenting on my paranoia, my brother and sister-in-law babysit my manuscripts on their computers.

The most famous stories of lost manuscripts involve train stations. T. E. Lawrence lost his manuscript of *The Seven Pillars of Wisdom* — all one thousand pages of it — while changing trains at Reading Station. He had previously destroyed all his working notes for it. And Hemingway's wife Hadley left a suitcase full of all his manuscripts, including the carbon copies, on a train platform while she went to buy a bottle of water.

Consider being paranoid about losing your own work.

The easiest thing about writing is backing up.

— ROB DALY

325. Clockwork Writers

Some writers can come up with books like clockwork — and these are not hack authors but fine writers who seem to find an endless source of creativity. We don't even want to think about Joyce Carol Oates's output. (Once I heard Carolyn See interviewing her, and Carolyn said, "Joyce, you can write faster than I can read.")

I'm in awe of Anne Tyler, who publishes a new novel every couple of years and has kept up this steady, orderly pace since the late seventies. Harlan Coben comes up with a best-selling thriller every single year. There are not exactly thousands of these writers, or even hundreds, but as for those who manage to consistently write and publish wonderful books, all we can do is admire them and try not to be too jealous.

It is so beautiful to live for many years with your story, while nobody else is knowing what are you doing, and in every moment you can pick up an idea or an image from your everyday experiences....I cannot understand these authors who concoct a new novel every year. Where is the fun, then?

— Umberto Eco

326. Danger

Take the *d* off *danger* and you've got *anger*. Both words contain adrenaline. You can write your way out of both.

I write out of my anger and into my passion.
— TERRY TEMPEST WILLIAMS

327. Money Problems and Bad Habits

To the people in his hometown of Oxford, Mississippi, William Faulkner appeared unemployed and "just another one of those crazy Faulkners with money problems and bad habits."

He was known as "Count No 'Count" until MGM showed up in town to film *Intruder in the Dust*.

Most of us will not have a movie company coming to town to film our novels, but when word gets around that we're writing, who knows what they'll say about our problems and habits.

The truth is that about 97 percent of "normal" people everywhere ...look on writing, if they look on it at all, as one step below whoredom. Because at least if you're a whore you're helping someone have a good time.

— CAROLYN SEE

328. Hope and Despair

Isak Dinesen said she wrote a little every day, without hope and without despair.

When asked about her process for writing poems, Tess Gallagher said that she "lights candles and invites the poems in" and faces "the coming or not-coming of the poem with neither hope nor despair."

I have to say that I personally don't know any writers who write without hope or despair, but if you can pull it off, you will probably be a much calmer writer than my friends and I.

Joyce Carol Oates says somewhere that when writers ask each other what time they start working and when they finish and how much time they take for lunch, they're actually trying to find out "Is he as crazy as I am?" I don't need that question answered.

— PHILIP ROTH

329. The Sacred Act

During writing exercises in class you can *hear* people writing
— the scratch of pens, the click-pat of computer keys. There's
such concentration and sweetness to the sound.

When students read what they've written about people
they've loved, friends and family, parents and grandparents —
especially those who are gone — I realize (again and again)
how sacred the act of putting stories into words on a page is.

So long as people read, those we loved survive however evanes-
cently. As do we writers, saying with our life's work, Remember.
Remember us. Remember me.

— MARGE PIERCY

330. The Frozen Sea

In 1903 Franz Kafka wrote to his friend Oskar Pollak: "I think we ought to read only the kind of books that wound and stab us. If the book we are reading doesn't wake us up with a blow on the head, what are we reading it for? ... We need the books that affect us like a disaster, that grieve us deeply, like the death of someone we loved more than ourselves, like being banished into forests far from everyone, like a suicide. A book must be the axe for the frozen sea inside us."

That last line of Kafka's letter has, of course, been quoted for over a century now.

Roger Rosenblatt says if it is true that a book can be an ax, then you must not forget that frozen sea when you write. You need to keep your reader in mind: "He flails in slow motion, palms pressed upward under the ice. Here's your ax.... And what do you get out of this act of rescue? You save two people: your reader and yourself."

For your writing to be great — and I mean great, not clever, or even brilliant, or most misleading of all, beautiful — it must be useful to the world.

— ROGER ROSENBLATT

331. Going Away to Write

There are degrees of going away to write: a summer on a remote island, a week in a cabin deep in the woods, or even one weekend with no one else in the house and the phone and email turned off. Or, more practically, a long walk with a notebook or an hour in a coffee shop. Even thirty minutes alone in your room with the door shut and a pencil in your hand can be thought of as going away.

We think of retreat as going away, but it need not be a physical act. Each of us can find our own way to silence. We withdraw and the inner world appears.

— DEENA METZGER

332. Editors

Hunter S. Thompson called editors "necessary evils" who helped to get him into print and who pointed out once in one of his manuscripts that it was impossible to sit in a hotel room in Milwaukee and look out at Lake Superior.

Peter Carey said he had an editor who "was always worrying about what was the rule for this and when did you do that." Speaking about this editor, Carey said, "I remember being on holiday in Provence and he was on the phone in the middle of the night talking for four hours about fucking ampersands. He was obsessed about the jacket design, he was obsessed with the selling and is very close to many booksellers. I was blessed."

I once had an editor who had a weekend place in the country, and when I was visiting my parents in a town nearby, Paula Diamond and I spent a week together sitting at her kitchen table editing the final draft of my novel. It was my first novel; I thought this was how editors operated. They supplied you with endless cups of coffee and went over every semicolon with you. Though I have loved and respected many editors since, not one of them has spent a week with me at their kitchen table discussing semicolons.

Many times over the years I have said to [my editor] things like: I will never speak to you again. Forever. Goodbye. That is it. Thank you very much. And I leave. Then I read the piece and I think of his suggestions. I send him a telegram that says, OK, so you're right.
— MAYA ANGELOU

333. What Discouraged Novelists Do

When her novel *Mansfield Park* was published, Jane Austen collected opinions about it from her family and friends and copied their comments down in a notebook. Some compared the novel unfavorably to *Pride and Prejudice*, and her brother Henry offered the opinion, still dreaded by writers, that it was "interesting." No one had a whole lot to say about it.

According to Carol Shields in her book about Austen: "She was disappointed in its reception. But she was already doing what any discouraged novelist does: She was beginning a new novel, *Emma*, which was to be a masterpiece."

Any writer, I suppose, feels that the world into which he was born is nothing less than a conspiracy against the cultivation of his talent.
— James Baldwin

334. Growing Plots with Green Apples

Raymond Chandler never plotted on paper; he did it in his head. He said, "Usually I do it wrong and have to do it all over again.... With me, plots are not made, they grow. And if they refuse to grow, you throw the stuff away and start over again."

When struggling with her plots, Agatha Christie would take a hot bath, eat green apples, and run the plot of her work in progress through her mind from start to finish.

Lawrence Durrell said that plotting was like driving a few stakes into the ground and then running ahead to plant another stake to show what direction you were going in.

Henry Green just let it come to him, page by page.

James Thurber believed that a writer shouldn't know too much about where he was going.

Within those successive drafts, my characters keep on doing the same things over and over; it's like some hellish repetition of events. But the reasons they do them gradually become more complex and layered and deeply rooted in the characters. Every day's a miracle: Wow, I did that, I didn't know any of that yesterday.

— PETER CAREY

335. A Month of Writing Selfishly

One month is left of this year devoted to your writing. One month to write, to polish, or to rev up the nerve to send your work out (if that's what you want to do) — thirty days of focus.

Be selfish. Hoard your time; know how precious your time really is.

A finished draft is a miracle.

I have been a selfish being all my life, in practice, though not in principle.

— JANE AUSTEN

336. Things Not Going Smoothly

Difficult times can happen to the best of writers. Here's an excerpt from Anton Chekhov's diary:

> October 17, 1896: "Performance of my 'Seagull' at the Alexandrinsky Theatre. It was not a success."
>
> December 4, 1896: "For the performance on the 17th October.... It is true that I fled from the theatre, but only when the play was over."

I've been working on my rewrite, that's right
I'm gonna change the ending

— PAUL SIMON

337. Letting the Critic Out

There will come a time to let your critic loose. When your work is ready to send out as a submission, all that carping about perfection can be invited in; that cold, critical eye can go to work finding the rambling paragraphs, the run-on sentences, the telling not showing, the generalizing, the murkiness, and the overuse of adjectives and adverbs. Because you're turning your writing into a pristine manuscript, whether you're sending it out in hard copy or by Internet, it will have good margins and white space; its pages will be numbered and double-spaced. What you're doing is sending your story out in its perfect little business suit to get the job.

You have no idea what a difference it makes for an over-read agent or editor to receive a beautiful-looking manuscript, printed cleanly on a laser printer in a nice, easy-to-read font with plenty of spacing.

— Noah Lukeman

338. Killing Your Darlings

You know those phrases we write that we love, full of feeling, beauty, and truth, etc.? Well, sometimes we have to kill them. We have to hit the Delete button because, beautiful as our words may be, those particular phrases or sentences or whole paragraphs just don't add a whole lot to the story. You've all heard the quote "You must kill your darlings."

Thomas Wolfe, whose editor, Max Perkins, famously had to cut *thousands* of words from Wolfe's rambling novels, said: "What I had to face, the very bitter lesson that everyone who wants to write has got to learn, was that a thing may in itself be the finest piece of writing one has ever done, and yet have absolutely no place in the manuscript one hopes to publish."

You don't always have to go so far as to murder your darlings.... But go back and look at them with a very beady eye. *Almost always it turns out that they'd be better dead.*

— DIANA ATHILL

339. Writers' Egos

As with most things, a sense of humor helps when you're a writer.

Bestselling author Pat Conroy accompanied his wife, Cassandra King, on her book tour, sitting off to the side as she autographed books. (He referred to himself as "Mr. Modesty.") A woman came up to him and said, "I just want to tell you that I came to this convention because of you....I have read every book you have ever written. I love your books. I've memorized pages of your books. I've always loved your books. But I don't think you'll ever write a better one than *Carrie*." He suddenly realized she had mistaken him for Stephen King, and later laughed as he told an interviewer the story.

But for every Pat Conroy there's a writer who throws a hissy fit because of a fragile ego when something goes off course. Avoid hissy fits at all costs; work on your sense of humor.

Your ego is a big, messy, undisciplined, anxiety-ridden dog. It barks and whines and pees on the floor and takes nips at passing strangers and goes crazy when it sees another dog that might be bigger or smarter or prettier.... The only thing you can do is try to keep it on a fairly short leash.

— CAROLYN SEE

340. Endings

I once spent a number of months weeping over a final chapter I was trying to write. I had sold the novel a year before and seriously hoped that if I gave back the advance, my publisher would just forget the whole thing. (This was the novel that ended up with a five-foot-tall pile of failed drafts.) Too much plot had to happen and be resolved in the last chapter — action and emotion, plus an attempted murder, for God's sake. So I cried and typed and moaned to everybody within earshot that I was going through torture and could never, ever pull off an ending for the damn book. But one day in July a whole bunch of little pieces started to fall into place, and lo and behold, the book had a rather good ending.

I hate endings. Just detest them. Beginnings are definitely the most exciting, middles are perplexing and endings are a disaster. The temptation towards resolution, towards wrapping up the package, seems to me a terrible trap. Why not be more honest with the moment? The most authentic endings are the ones which are already revolving towards another beginning.

— SAM SHEPARD

341. The Dog Ate It

Jack Kerouac wrote *On the Road* on long scrolls of paper so he wouldn't have to pause to insert a new page into the typewriter. He said he went fast because the road was fast. At the end of the original manuscript, on a scroll of twelve feet, he wrote a note by hand: "DOG ATE (Potchky — a dog)."

There was speculation that he didn't like his original ending and tore it up himself. Others thought that he couldn't come up with an ending, so he came up with the dog story.

The writing is dewlike, everything happens as it really did. . . . Jack needs, however, an ending.

— ALLEN GINSBERG

342. Going Down the Chute

Tina Fey warns about being too precious with your work; you have to try your hardest to do your best but then let go. "You can't be that kid standing at the top of the waterslide, over-thinking it," she says. "You have to go down the chute."

And for writers, going down the chute means slapping something on the page, letting it sit there in all of its dreadful-ness while you forge onward. We always want to try to make it perfect, but you'll sit there forever agonizing over one sentence, one paragraph, one page if you don't let go. You can always come back to it and rewrite, but move on, go down the chute to the next page, the next chapter.

And sometimes it means clicking the Send button.

Yes, you're going to write some sketches that you love and are proud of forever — your golden nuggets. But you're also going to write some real shit nuggets. You can't worry about it.

— TINA FEY

343. Pressing the Send Button

Work used to be sent out in large envelopes, with self-addressed stamped envelopes (SASEs) accompanying a story or essay or poems. And if you sent out a complete book manuscript, it would go into a box for mailing. All of this felt right — action was involved, packaging, labeling, trips to the post office. But now most agents and editors want electronic copies. So you sit there alone in your room or office or kitchen, or wherever you work, with your mouse pointer hovering over the Send button. One click, and a book, an essay, a story, goes down the chute into cyberspace.

I ordered a glass of white wine and two scoops of toffee ice cream. I looked at everyone, spoke to no one, and kept smiling: "I've finished a book. Soon maybe I can be a human being again."
— Natalie Goldberg

344. Naked on the Street

Sending your work out into the world, hoping an editor will love it, buy it, and publish it, is not unlike walking out the front door stark naked and strolling down the street in broad daylight. This is your life, your innermost thoughts and dreams and beliefs, your imagination, out there for everyone to read, perhaps sneer at, laugh at, reject. Quite possibly these may be your thoughts when you seal the envelope or click the Send button. (On the other hand, if you're puffed up with total confidence, you might want to dial it down a bit.)

Realize that there are editors out there hoping your story, your essay, your book is wonderful. Their jobs exist because writers exist. They need us every bit as much as we need them. Part of your job is to look for publications, publishing houses, editors, and agents who would be interested in your subject and style of writing. In other words, do your homework. Know who you're sending your work to and know what they've previously published or, if agents, what authors they handle.

A person who publishes a book will fully appear before the populace with his pants down.

— EDNA ST. VINCENT MILLAY

345. The Marketing Whore/Pimp

Publish means "to make public." You can publish online and have your writing forever lodged in cyberspace; you can publish via your own printer and hand out copies to your friends; you can try to get a publishing house or periodical to buy your work, and they handle it all; or you can self-publish through a company that does publishing on demand, and you pay them to create the book for you. Whatever you end up doing, if you want people to read what you've written, you will become your own marketing person, otherwise known as a Marketing Whore (or Pimp).

If it's a book you get published, you will now be thinking of ordering postcards featuring a jacket photo of your book that you will mail or hand to every living, breathing person you know or come into contact with. You will troll for friends on Facebook, you will have a blog and a website, you will create long address lists and do email blasts. You will dial for dates at bookstores. You will tweet and toot your own horn. If you should find any of this a lot of fun, you might think of going into advertising instead of writing.

Writing is like prostitution. First you do it for love, and then you do it for a few close friends, and then for the money.

— Molière

346. How to Get an Agent

We find our luck sometimes by not thinking things through — by being impetuous and risking making a fool of ourselves. Which is how I got an agent. I sent a bunch of my poems to Garson Kanin — the director and writer who had given me my first Broadway acting job. If I had thought it through, been smarter and calmer, I would never have popped a few dozen of my angst-in-suburbia poems off to Mr. Kanin (as I always called him). However, generous man that he was, he wrote me back a charming letter complimenting me on the poems and suggesting that I get an agent. He had one in mind who was just starting out. Now trust me when I tell you that no agent on the face of this planet, just starting out or otherwise, is eager to have a poet as a client, especially one with absolutely no publishing track record. (Other than a dirty novel, which I didn't mention.) However, the fledgling agent didn't want to alienate Garson Kanin, so he got in touch with me; and when he heard I was also writing a novel, he got a little more interested. Five years and two failed novels later, he sold my first book.

This is not really about how to get an agent. It's about following your instincts, not your brain.

Trust your instincts. And never hope more than you work.
— RITA MAE BROWN

347. Good Company

Here are a few stories to remember, should you feel defeated if your work is rejected:

Susanna Moore's first novel was turned down by an agent who suggested that she find another line of work. The novel was eventually nominated for a National Book Award. James Michener's agent lost faith in him and quit just before Michener won the Pulitzer Prize for *Tales of the South Pacific*. Another eventual Pulitzer Prize winner, Robert Olen Butler, had twenty editors reject his novel; but some of them had praised it at the same time, so he didn't give up. Norman Mailer's *The Naked and the Dead* was turned down by one editor who wrote, "In my opinion it is barely publishable." An early manuscript by Emily Dickinson was dismissed as "generally devoid of true poetical qualities." And it would be hard to beat this response that Ernest Hemingway received for *The Torrents of Spring*: "It would be in extremely rotten taste, to say nothing of being horribly cruel, should we want to publish it."

It's not personal. It's not death. It's just a death experience. And the way to defuse rejection is to turn it into a process: cosmic badminton.

— CAROLYN SEE

348. Walking Dogs and Staying Sane

Does writing keep us sane? John Jerome questioned this, echoing Joy Williams, in a book he wrote about a year in his life as a freelancer. "How sane is it to sit alone in a room, fashioning sentences for as many hours a day as one can stand to sit there? And thereby lose complete contact with the very room you sit in, not to mention the world outside, the real world, your putative life? Maybe it is the writing that keeps us crazy."

While I think he makes a very good, logical argument for this, I believe that writing keeps us sane.

I do agree, though, when he talks about another path to sanity: "the walking cure." He writes, "Our two dogs accompany me.... Maybe it's actually the dogs that keep me sane."

I have been accustomed to taking long daily walks with my dog Aquinnah. Our walks are for business and for pleasure, and also for survival — interlocking motives that have somehow acquired nearly equal importance in my mind. Without a daily walk and the transactions it stimulates in my head, I would face the first page of cold blank paper with pitiful anxiety.

— WILLIAM STYRON

349. What's in a Name

Margaret Mitchell intended that the book she was writing in bits and pieces from 1925 to 1935 would be entitled *Tomorrow Is Another Day*. Her second choice for a title was *Tote the Weary Load*.

Happily for all concerned, it was published under a third title: *Gone with the Wind*.

A good title should be like a good metaphor; it should intrigue without being too baffling or too obvious.

— WALKER PERCY

350. Pride and Prejudice

Jane Austen's brother claimed that "everything came finished from her pen." That's pretty much how we imagine all great writers do it — their work flows directly, easily, happily, *finished*, from their pen or computer, to pristine manuscript pages, to their published books. However, this is not true of any of the writers I know and apparently was not true of Jane Austen, either. A professor at Oxford University discovered that Austen's handwritten pages were a mess, with grammatical errors, omissions, and often nonexistent punctuation. What Jane Austen had was a very good editor.

A good editor is right up there with God as your copilot. A good editor can envision your work going farther than you ever imagined. A good editor keeps you from making ghastly mistakes in judgment and in grammar. A good editor makes you think whatever changes are made were all your idea.

A bad editor will change the sound of your voice on the page; a good one will help you find it.

You know the part between page 18 and 92? Well let's make it into one very good sentence.

— MICHAEL KORDA

351. The Woo-Woos of Publishing

Let's say you finish your first draft, then you go on to write a second draft and however many more are necessary, and finally you publish your book. This is indeed deserving of cheers and congratulations. But one night after you do a reading in a bookstore and are signing copies of your book (be prepared — it might be a short line), someone will come up who hasn't actually bought your book and say something that will give you pause. She will tell you she was studying your chakras as you read — and, well, you have trouble; your chakras are blocked, she'll say. You will look at her, and you will be very tired, and for one minute you'll believe that this stranger with her woo-woo weirdness might be on to all the unresolved issues in your life. And you will suddenly get very depressed and want to stab her with your pen. But you won't. However, the joy of publishing will have now reached realistic levels.

I tell you, if what you have in mind is fame and fortune, publication is going to drive you crazy.

— ANNE LAMOTT

352. Another Bookstore Story

Jennie Nash and I were making a joint bookstore appearance at a big bookstore in a huge mall. Our books were on a similar subject, breast cancer, and were coming out at the same time. We were good friends, and our editors in New York knew each other. In their infinite wisdom they thought we should do, well, kind of a "cancer night" together. I felt the first drumbeats of possible disaster when I read the bookstore flyer — "COME SHARE YOUR STORY OF CANCER!" But never mind. I loved Jennie, and what fun to do an evening together, even if it was to be a cancer evening. We arrived at the bookstore, and they were ready for us with huge stacks of our books and rows of chairs for our audience. How pleased and flattered we were!

One woman arrived. And then my friend Bonnie showed up, immediately doubling the size of the audience. That was it.

The poor woman who had come, thinking she'd hide quietly in the back row, got our full attention and energy for the evening, and though we gave her our email and website addresses, we never heard from her again.

I belong to a vanishing breed that thinks a writer should be read and not heard, let alone seen.

— WILLIAM GADDIS

353. But Then...

There will be other times when you read from your book in a bookstore or at a literary event and you can feel the connection to your audience. When they laugh in the right places or are silent and attentive when you hope they will be. And they ask lively and engaged questions during the Q and A, and afterward they come up to tell you their own stories. And no one comments on your blocked chakras.

I have spent the last year with wonderful strangers, dog people from every corner of this country who want to tell me their stories. They have shown up at readings...with letters and photos.

— PAM HOUSTON

354. How to Lighten Up about Reviews

I read the early reviews of one of my books, an anthology of essays, online, and one reviewer basically tried to rewrite the book for me. Another had found two grammatical errors in her uncorrected proof copy and seemed to be very angry about it. The funniest, in retrospect, was the reviewer who thought the book would have been much better if it had been written not by writers but by "real" people. There were also some really wonderful reviews. But here's something you'll learn or might already know — the reviews you will remember verbatim are the negative ones.

For about twenty-four hours I was depressed about the bad reviews, and then I checked books that I loved to see if they ever got bad reviews on this site. Lo and behold, my favorite book on writing memoir got one review that was so negative ("not worth the paper printed on") that it gave me perspective on the whole review thing. And the best part of all, there was a comment to the review, and it was from the author herself. She wrote, "Oh, my goodness, maybe you should ask for your money back."

The really positive ones are boring after a while — your own most generous self-appraisal quoted back to you — but I must admit I find bad reviews fascinating. They're like the proverbial train wreck, only you're in the train; will all those mangled bodies at the bottom of the ravine tell you something unexpected about yourself?
— DAVID SHIELDS

355. Planning the Next Day's Work

Beatrice Wood discovered pottery when she was forty years old, and it changed her life; she became an artist. She also became a writer in her late eighties and published a number of books, including a hilarious and inspiring memoir of hard work, a deep spiritual quest, wild love affairs, and delicious gossip. I met her once when she was 104 years old; she was dressed in her trademark silk sari and heavy jewelry and was still working. Every day, she went to her studio to make art, right up to the end of her life a year later.

"At night I lie in bed," she wrote in her memoir, "and plan my next day of work in the studio. I imagine the bowls, chalices, tiles I will create."

I would not say I had great gifts as a potter, but I organized myself to become one....I was the hardest working. In the end, it is only hard work that counts.

— BEATRICE WOOD

356. Publicity and Pianos

A grand piano suddenly appeared on a sandbar in Florida. Sitting on a tiny spot in the middle of Biscayne Bay, this lone piano was on the evening news, in the papers, and on the Internet. How did it get there? It turned out that a teenager wanting to make an impression in order to get accepted into art school had taken the old piano out of his grandmother's garage, sailed it on the family boat to the sandbar, set it on fire, and had pictures taken of himself pretending to play it as it burned.

I'm not suggesting that you plant pianos in unlikely places and set them on fire to get attention, but you might think up innovative ways to get people to notice your work.

A boy has to peddle his book.

— TRUMAN CAPOTE

357. When It's Impossible to Write

There will come a morning, a week — sometimes a whole month or so — when it simply feels impossible to write. Your head starts to buzz with anxiety just looking at your computer.

Here in a nutshell is some of the best advice I know for this situation. It comes from Richard Rhodes: "If writing a book is impossible, write a chapter. If writing a chapter is impossible, write a page. If writing a page is impossible, write a paragraph. If writing a paragraph is impossible, write a sentence. If writing even a sentence is impossible, write a word and teach yourself everything there is to know about that word and then write another, connected word and see where their connection leads."

Remember you love writing. It wouldn't be worth it if you didn't. If the love fades, do what you need to do and get back to it.

— A. L. KENNEDY

358. Grand Gestures of Renunciation

When she was about to turn forty, Madeleine L'Engle couldn't find a publisher for her now-classic children's books *A Wrinkle in Time* (editors were concerned that it dealt with evil) and *Meet the Austins* (it opened with a death). But she also had a novel for adults that was being seriously considered by an editor, and her hopes were high for getting it accepted. On her fortieth birthday she found out that the adult novel had been rejected. She took this as a sign, and with guilt (all that time she'd spent writing, away from her children!) and many tears, she "covered the typewriter with a grand gesture of renunciation." But as she was sobbing, she realized her subconscious mind was working on a novel about failure.

She uncovered the typewriter and kept writing.

I had to write. I had no choice in the matter. It was not up to me to say I would stop, because I could not. It didn't matter how small or inadequate my talent. If I never had another book published, and it was clear to me that this was a real possibility, I still had to go on writing.

— MADELEINE L'ENGLE

359. The Spirit Line

You never get to the end of your stories. The need to figure it out, make sense of things, keep track. Just when you think you've nailed an experience, put it all down, created order out of chaos, created something manageable on paper with the nuts and bolts of your life, a new loss, a new joy, a new idea or question will crash in.

Gail Caldwell writes about the old Navajo weavers who used to include an intentional flaw in their rugs called a spirit line, which was meant to lead the way to a new beginning, the next creation.

Every story in life worth holding on to has to have a spirit line. You can call this hope or tomorrow or the "and then" of narrative itself.
— GAIL CALDWELL

360. On Not Giving Up

Kathryn Stockett got sixty rejections for her bestselling novel *The Help*. Her first rejection read, "Story did not sustain my interest." But it was her very first rejection, so she was actually thrilled with it — a real rejection letter! She went back to editing her book. Her fortieth rejection finally made her cry. It read, "There is no market for this kind of tiring writing."

She wouldn't give up, though, and she began lying to her friends and family, sneaking off to hotels to secretly work on the novel. Finally, after five years, the sixty-first response she received was from an agent who loved the book and sold it three weeks later.

The point is, I can't tell you how to succeed. But I can tell you how not to: Give in to the shame of being rejected and put your manuscript — or painting, song, voice, dance moves... in the coffin that is your bedside drawer and close it for good.

— KATHRYN STOCKETT

361. The Sum of This Year

You have some stories or essays now, or your first draft in some stage of completion. Or maybe you have a pile of scribbled pages or notebooks, or a computer file full of notes.

Give yourself credit for anything you've written this year. Turn on your sweetheart voice, and let it tell you how brave you've been to write anything at all.

And then figure out what you're going to do with your manuscript or notes.

Don't give yourself the excuse of feeling overwhelmed. You've come this far; now get on with it.

Finish what you're writing. Whatever you have to do to finish it, finish it.

— NEIL GAIMAN

362. Writing as Practice

You don't perform yoga; you practice it — with patience, trying for some humility. The same with religion or a path of spirituality, and also with writing. You practice writing; you don't perform it (until that day you start playing Marketing Whore/Pimp, which really has nothing to do with writing).

Practicing, that's all you're doing when you write.

Every day, take a deep breath and practice.

You may wish to change your life, you may be in therapy or religion, but your new vision remains merely talk until it enters the practice of your day.

— JOHN O'DONOHUE

363. The Secret to Life

"Now that you're eighty, you must know the secret of life," Donald Hall once said to Henry Moore. "What is the secret of life?" And the great sculptor replied: "The secret to life is to have a task, something you devote your entire life to, something you bring everything to, every minute of the day for your whole life. And the most important thing is — it must be something you cannot possibly do!"

Aren't we all trying to turn our writing into the perfection of art, something that the vast majority of us can't possibly achieve? But to have a task like this, to love writing and books, to simply be part of the energy of trying for that high road of literature and never giving up on it — this is the secret to life for a writer.

Whether you succeed or not is irrelevant, there is no such thing. Making your unknown is the important thing — and keeping the unknown always beyond you. Catching, crystallizing your simpler, clearer vision of life — only to see it turn stale compared to what you vaguely feel ahead — that you must always keep working to grasp.

— Georgia O'Keeffe

364. Moving toward Grace

A student emails me this message: "I will expect everything, the bad writing, the stuck feeling, the boredom, but I'll know that there will be moments of grace where I am more alive and engaged when writing than in any other creative endeavor that I do, and the more simple the habit I develop, the more chance of having those moments of grace, and to just know that regardless of what happens today, tomorrow I will be moving my pen across the page."

The trick is not in becoming *a writer, it is in* staying *a writer. Day after week after month after year.*

— HARLAN ELLISON

365. Remember This

And have you written toward your own moments of grace? Have you taken risks and gone from safe places into danger in order to write what you need to write?

Did you dive into the past and write the things you were told never to air in public? Did you find some humor in the chaos of your life? Did you write during the days and months when your head felt empty and you had doubts? Did you get something on the page? Because that's all we can ask for and expect every day — something on the page.

Remember that you have a story to tell that no one else on earth can tell the same way you can.

Remember that your story is important; someone needs to read it.

Remember what a connected community you're part of when you write.

Remember that you can find the most inspiring teachers in every book you love.

Remember that you can be awash in doubt and fear and still write.

Remember that the way out of doubt and fear is through them, one word after another.

Fifty-Two Weeks of Writing Prompts

Giving yourself a tight time limit for writing exercises is like having a mini-deadline — it creates pressure, gets you moving. When using any of these prompts, try writing for five minutes without pausing. (Of course, if you get on a roll, just keep going.) Most of the following prompts can be used for either fiction or for memoir and essays. If you're writing fiction, just substitute a character's name for "you."

Don't spend a lot of time thinking about these prompts; just start writing and figure it out on paper as you go — surprise yourself.

1. What is your own metaphor for fear of writing that first line? Imagine a landscape or animal or weather or music or whatever springs to mind.
2. Write a letter (but don't mail it) to someone close to you about your first chapter, essay, or short story.
3. Write about a time you got caught.

4. Write about a time you were disappointed.
5. Write about a time you were in a jam.
6. Write about trying to bluff your way through.
7. Write about a time you were naked and uncomfortable.
8. Write about a time you were naked and very happy.
9. Write about your worst failure.
10. Write about an animal you have or once had. Or write about not wanting an animal.
11. Write a list of ways to nurture your writing.
12. Write about why you want to write.
13. Write about a time you dug your heels in and got stubborn.
14. Write about the cool kids club in high school.
15. Write the story of your life in five minutes.
16. Write your first memory.
17. Take your notebook to a public place and spy. Write down what you see and hear.
18. Write an opening to a story based on what you wrote for prompt 17.
19. Write about a time you felt like a beginner at something.
20. Write about a lie you once told.
21. Write about a time you didn't show up.
22. Write about a time you were frightened.
23. Write about forgiving somebody for something you never thought you could forgive.
24. Write about something that makes your hands sweat.
25. Write about your name — where you got it, how you feel about it.
26. Write about a binge that you or someone you know went on.
27. Write about a gift you received and lied about liking.
28. Write about a time you broke something.

29. Write about a time you hit a wall.

30. Write about your favorite pair of shoes when you were a kid.

31. Write about your current favorite pair of shoes.

32. Write down the word "perfection" and then whatever words come into your head.

33. Write about a memory from childhood that only you and your family know.

34. Write about a time you felt guilty.

35. Write about learning — or not learning — to swim.

36. Write about a raft, metaphoric or literal.

37. Write about a key, metaphoric or literal.

38. Write about a time you got approval — or didn't.

39. Write about a teacher or mentor who changed your life, for either good or bad.

40. Write down a list of words you love.

41. Start a story using the words from prompt 40.

42. Write about a time you had to wing it.

43. Write about what you'd attempt to do if you knew you could not fail.

44. Write about your own giant block of whatever is most difficult for you.

45. Write about the most dangerous place you know.

46. Write about a time you fell on your face.

47. Start with "Once upon a time..." and write your life as a fairy tale.

48. Write about four things that never change.

49. Write about your father's hands.

50. Write about losing something and then finding it.

51. Write about a time you stepped up to the plate.

52. Write down two or three things you know for sure.

Acknowledgments

Thanks to:

My agent, Lisa Erbach Vance, for being so smart, patient, tenacious, and such a good friend. And to everyone at the Aaron M. Priest Literary Agency, especially and always, Aaron and Arleen.

My editor, the wonderful Jason Gardner, for being a joy to work with, and the whole talented, dedicated crew at New World Library: Mark Colucci, copyeditor extraordinaire, Kristen Cashman, Monique Muhlenkamp, Munro Magruder, Tracy Cunningham, and Tona Pearce-Myers.

My posse of early readers: Billy Mernit, who said of course this had to be day by day and later went over it page by page and kept me from embarrassing myself; Carol Perkins, whose insightful and cheery notes kept me going during bad days; Sally Court, whose early conviction and encouragement got the book going in the first place; and Rob Daly, who reads with a meticulous eye and also saves me from computer hell.

My friend Linda Venis, director of the Writers' Program at UCLA Extension, for creating such an amazing community of writers, both instructors and students. And to her staff, who make the logistics of teaching so easy.

My family: R., who lets me steal his best lines; my beautiful daughters, who gave me the incomparable Emma, Axel, and Grace; and Bill and Diane Mattes, who babysat countless drafts of this book on their computers.

My students, without whom there would be no book. I'm especially grateful to those who gave me permission to use their experiences or to quote them directly, and also to those who gave me articles, online sources, and ideas for this book.

Bibliography

Ackerman, Diane. *One Hundred Names for Love: A Stroke, a Marriage, and the Language of Healing*. New York: Norton, 2011.

Allende, Isabel. *The Sum of Our Days*. Translated by Margaret Sayers Peden. New York: Harper Perennial, 2009.

Allison, Dorothy. *Two or Three Things I Know for Sure*. New York: Plume, 1996.

Alvarez, Julia. *Something to Declare*. New York: Plume, 1998.

Andreas, Brian. *Traveling Light: Stories & Drawings for a Quiet Mind*. Decorah, IA: StoryPeople, 2005.

Angelou, Maya. *Letter to My Daughter*. New York: Random House, 2008.

Arana, Marie, ed. *The Writing Life: Writers on How They Think and Work*. New York: PublicAffairs, 2003.

Atwood, Margaret. *Negotiating with the Dead: A Writer on Writing*. Cambridge: Cambridge University Press, 2002.

Baker, Nicholson. *U and I: A True Story*. New York: Random House, 1991.

Baldwin, Christina. *Storycatcher: Making Sense of Our Lives through the Power and Practice of Story*. Novato, CA: New World Library, 2005.

Baszile, Jennifer. *The Black Girl Next Door: A Memoir*. New York: Simon & Schuster, 2009.

Bayles, David, and Ted Orland. *Art & Fear: Observations on the Perils (and Rewards) of Artmaking*. Santa Cruz, CA: Image Continuum Press, 2001.

Bernard, André. *Now All We Need Is a Title: Famous Book Titles and How They Got That Way*. New York: Norton, 1996.

————, ed. *Rotten Rejections: A Literary Companion*. Wainscott, NY: Pushcart Press, 1990.

Bernstein, Harry. *The Invisible Wall: A Love Story That Broke Barriers*. New York: Ballantine Books, 2007.

Bloom, Claire. *Leaving a Doll's House: A Memoir*. New York: Little, Brown, 1996.

Blythe, Will, ed. *Why I Write: Thoughts on the Craft of Fiction*. Boston: Little, Brown, 1998.

Bradbury, Ray. *Zen in the Art of Writing: Essays on Creativity*. Santa Barbara, CA: Capra Press, 1990.

Brande, Dorothea. *Becoming a Writer*. New York: Harcourt, Brace, 1934. Reprinted with foreword by John Gardner. New York: Tarcher, 1981.

Brodie, Deborah, ed. *Writing Changes Everything: The 627 Best Things Anyone Ever Said about Writing*. New York: St. Martin's Press, 1997.

Brown, Rita Mae. *Starting from Scratch: A Different Kind of Writer's Manual*. New York: Bantam Books, 1988.

Buechner, Frederick. *The Sacred Journey: A Memoir of Early Days*. San Francisco: HarperSanFrancisco, 1982.

Carlson, Ron. *Ron Carlson Writes a Story*. Saint Paul, MN: Graywolf Press, 2007.

Casey, Maud. "A Life in Books." In *Mentors, Muses & Monsters: 30 Writers on the People Who Changed Their Lives*, edited by Elizabeth Benedict. New York: Free Press, 2009.

Chai, May-lee. Hapa *Girl: A Memoir*. Philadelphia: Temple University Press, 2007.

Checkoway, Julie, ed. *Creating Fiction: Instruction and Insights from Teachers of the Associated Writing Programs*. Cincinnati: Story Press, 1999.

Chekhov, Anton. *Notebook of Anton Chekhov*. Translated by S. S. Koteliansky and Leonard Woolf. New York: Ecco Press, 1987.

Conrad, Barnaby, and the staff of the Santa Barbara Writers' Conference, eds. *The Complete Guide to Writing Fiction*. Cincinnati: Writer's Digest Books, 1990.

Couric, Katie, ed. *The Best Advice I Ever Got: Lessons from Extraordinary Lives*. New York: Random House, 2011.

Csikszentmihalyi, Mihaly. *Flow: The Psychology of Optimal Experience*. New York: Harper & Row, 1990.

de Botton, Alain. "On Writing." In *Finding the Words: Writers on Inspiration*,

Desire, War, Celebrity, Exile, and Breaking the Rules, edited by Jared Bland. Toronto: McClelland & Stewart, 2011.

Dennis, Sandy. *Sandy Dennis: A Personal Memoir*. Edited by Louise Ladd and Doug Taylor. Watsonville, CA: Papier-Mache Press, 1997.

Dillard, Annie. *Pilgrim at Tinker Creek*. New York: Harper's Magazine Press, 1974.

————. *The Writing Life*. New York: Harper & Row, 1989.

Doty, Mark. *The Art of Description: World into Word*. Minneapolis: Graywolf Press, 2010.

————. *Heaven's Coast: A Memoir*. New York: HarperCollins, 1996.

————. *Still Life with Oysters and Lemon*. Boston: Beacon Press, 2001.

Dubus, Andre. *Meditations from a Movable Chair*. New York: Vintage Books, 1999.

Epel, Naomi. *Writers Dreaming*. New York: Carol Southern Books, 1993.

Fairfax, John, and John Moat. *The Way to Write: A Stimulating Guide to the Craft of Creative Writing*. New York: St. Martin's Press, 1981.

Fey, Tina. *Bossypants*. New York: Little, Brown, 2011.

Findley, Timothy. *Inside Memory: Pages from a Writer's Workbook*. Toronto: HarperCollins, 1990.

Finnamore, Suzanne. *Split: A Memoir of Divorce*. New York: Dutton, 2008.

Flaherty, Alice W. *The Midnight Disease: The Drive to Write, Writer's Block, and the Creative Brain*. Boston: Houghton Mifflin, 2004.

Freed, Lynn. *Reading, Writing, and Leaving Home: Life on the Page*. Orlando, FL: Harcourt, 2005.

Friedman, Bonnie. *Writing Past Dark: Envy, Fear, Distraction, and Other Dilemmas in the Writer's Life*. New York: HarperCollins, 1993.

Friedman, Ellen G., ed. *Joan Didion: Essays & Conversations*. Princeton, NJ: Ontario Review Press, 1984.

Gilchrist, Ellen. *Falling through Space: The Journals of Ellen Gilchrist*. Boston: Little, Brown, 1987.

Ginzburg, Natalia. *The Little Virtues*. Translated by Dick Davis. New York: Arcade, 1989.

Goldberg, Natalie. *Old Friend from Far Away: The Practice of Writing Memoir*. New York: Free Press, 2007.

————. *Writing Down the Bones: Freeing the Writer Within*. Boston: Shambhala, 1986.

Gordon, Mary. "Putting Pen to Paper; but Not Just Any Pen or Just Any Paper." In New York Times, *Writers on Writing: Collected Essays from the New York Times*.

Gornick, Vivian. *The Situation and the Story: The Art of Personal Narrative*. New York: Farrar, Straus and Giroux, 2001.

Grumbach, Doris. *Life in a Day*. Boston: Beacon Press, 1990.

Hall, Donald, ed. *The Oxford Book of Literary Anecdotes*. Oxford: Oxford University Press, 1981.

Hall, Oakley. *The Art & Craft of Novel Writing*. Cincinnati: Story Press, 1989.

Halpern, Daniel, ed. *Our Private Lives: Journals, Notebooks, and Diaries*. New York: Vintage Books, 1990.

Hathaway, Katharine Butler. *The Little Locksmith: A Memoir*. New York: Feminist Press, 2000.

Heffron, Jack, ed. *The Best Writing on Writing*. Cincinnati: Story Press, 1994.

Hemingway, Ernest. *A Moveable Feast*. New York: Scribner, 1964.

Horgan, Paul. *Approaches to Writing*. 2nd ed. Middletown, CT: Wesleyan University Press, 1988.

Isherwood, Christopher. *The Sixties: Diaries. Vol. 2, 1960–1969*. Edited by Katherine Bucknell. New York: Harper, 2010.

Jerome, John. *The Writing Trade: A Year in the Life*. New York: Viking, 1992.

Johnson, Alexandra. *Leaving a Trace: On Keeping a Journal; The Art of Transforming a Life into Stories*. Boston: Little, Brown, 2001.

Karr, Mary. *Lit: A Memoir*. New York: HarperCollins, 2009.

Keaton, Diane. *Then Again*. New York: Random House, 2011.

Keen, Sam, and Anne Valley-Fox. *Your Mythic Journey: Finding Meaning in Your Life through Writing and Storytelling*. Los Angeles: Tarcher, 1989.

Keillor, Garrison, ed. *Good Poems for Hard Times*. New York: Viking, 2005.

Kenyon, Jane. *Otherwise: New and Selected Poems*. Saint Paul, MN: Graywolf Press, 1996.

Keyes, Ralph. *The Courage to Write: How Writers Transcend Fear*. New York: Henry Holt, 1995.

———. *The Writer's Book of Hope: Getting from Frustration to Publication*. New York: Henry Holt, 2003.

King, Stephen. *On Writing: A Memoir of the Craft*. New York: Scribner, 2000.

Kingsolver, Barbara. *High Tide in Tucson: Essays from Now or Never*. New York: HarperCollins, 1995.

Kingston, Maxine Hong. *To Be the Poet*. Cambridge, MA: Harvard University Press, 2002.

Kittredge, William. *Hole in the Sky: A Memoir*. New York: Vintage Books, 1993.

Knapp, Caroline. *Pack of Two: The Intricate Bond between People and Dogs*. New York: Dial Press, 1998.

Kooser, Ted. *Lights on a Ground of Darkness: An Evocation of a Place and Time*. Lincoln: University of Nebraska Press, 2005.

Kooser, Ted, and Steve Cox. *Writing Brave & Free: Encouraging Words for*

People Who Want to Start Writing. Lincoln: University of Nebraska Press, 2006.

Krementz, Jill. *The Writer's Desk*. New York: Random House, 1996.

Lawson, Lewis A., and Victor A. Kramer, eds. *Conversations with Walker Percy*. Jackson: University Press of Mississippi, 1985.

L'Engle, Madeleine. *A Circle of Quiet*. New York: HarperOne, 1972.

————. *Madeleine L'Engle Herself: Reflections on a Writing Life*. Compiled by Carole F. Chase. Colorado Springs: Shaw Books, 2001.

Lindbergh, Anne Morrow. *Gift from the Sea*. New York: Pantheon Books, 2005.

Lukeman, Noah. *The First Five Pages: A Writer's Guide to Staying out of the Rejection Pile*. New York: Simon & Schuster, 2000.

Maclean, Norman. *A River Runs through It and Other Stories*. Chicago: University of Chicago Press, 2001.

May, Rollo. *The Courage to Create*. New York: Norton, 1975.

McKee, Robert. *Story: Substance, Structure, Style, and the Principles of Screenwriting*. New York: HarperCollins, 1997.

McMorris, Megan, ed. *Woman's Best Friend: Women Writers on the Dogs in Their Lives*. Emeryville, CA: Seal Press, 2006.

McMurtry, Larry. *Film Flam: Essays on Hollywood*. New York: Simon & Schuster, 1987.

————. *Literary Life: A Second Memoir*. New York: Simon & Schuster, 2009.

Mernit, Billy. *Writing the Romantic Comedy: From "Cute Meet" to "Joyous Defeat"; How to Write Screenplays That Will Sell*. New York: HarperResource, 2000.

Metzger, Deena. *Writing for Your Life: A Guide and Companion to the Inner Worlds*. San Francisco: HarperSanFrancisco, 1992.

Miller, Sue. "Virtual Reality: The Perils of Seeking a Novelist's Facts in Her Fiction." In New York Times, *Writers on Writing: Collected Essays from the New York Times*.

Morrison, Toni. "The Art of Fiction No. 134." *Paris Review* 128 (Fall 1993). Accessed November 20, 2011. www.theparisreview.org/interviews/1888/the-art-of-fiction-no-134-toni-morrison.

Mosley, Walter. "For Authors, Fragile Ideas Need Loving Every Day." In New York Times, *Writers on Writing: Collected Essays from the New York Times*.

————. *This Year You Write Your Novel*. New York: Little, Brown, 2007.

Moyers, Bill. *Fooling with Words: A Celebration of Poets and Their Craft*. New York: Morrow, 1999.

————. *A World of Ideas: Conversations with Thoughtful Men and Women about American Life Today and the Ideas Shaping Our Future*. New York: Doubleday, 1990.

Murakami, Haruki. *What I Talk about When I Talk about Running: A Memoir*. Translated by Philip Gabriel. New York: Vintage International, 2009.

Nash, Jennie. *The Victoria's Secret Catalog Never Stops Coming: And Other Lessons I Learned from Breast Cancer*. New York: Scribner, 2003.

Newlove, Donald. *First Paragraphs: Inspired Openings for Writers and Readers*. New York: St. Martin's Press, 1992.

New York Times. *Writers on Writing: Collected Essays from the New York Times*. New York: Times Books, 2001.

————. *Writers on Writing*. Vol. 2, *More Collected Essays from the New York Times*. New York: Times Books, 2003.

Norris, Kathleen. *Amazing Grace: A Vocabulary of Faith*. New York: Riverhead Books, 1998.

————. *Dakota: A Spiritual Geography*. Boston: Houghton Mifflin, 2001.

Nunez, Sigrid. *Sempre Susan: A Memoir of Susan Sontag*. New York: Atlas, 2011.

O'Donohue, John. *Anam Cara: A Book of Celtic Wisdom*. New York: Cliff Street Books, 1997.

Olds, Sharon. *The Wellspring: Poems*. New York: Knopf, 1996.

Oliver, Mary. *Blue Pastures*. New York: Harcourt Brace, 1995.

————. *New and Selected Poems*. Boston: Beacon Press, 1992.

————. *A Poetry Handbook*. New York: Harcourt Brace, 1994.

Palumbo, Dennis. *Writing from the Inside Out: Transforming Your Psychological Blocks to Release the Writer Within*. New York: Wiley, 2000.

Parker, James. "The Last Pop Star." *Atlantic Magazine*, June 2010.

Piercy, Marge. *Sleeping with Cats: A Memoir*. New York: Morrow, 2002.

Plimpton, George, ed. *The Writer's Chapbook: A Compendium of Fact, Opinion, Wit, and Advice from the 20th Century's Preeminent Writers*. New York: Viking, 1989.

Prose, Francine. *Reading Like a Writer: A Guide for People Who Love Books and for Those Who Want to Write Them*. New York: HarperCollins, 2006.

Rechy, John. *About My Life and the Kept Woman: A Memoir*. New York: Grove Press, 2008.

Reeves, Judy. *A Writer's Book of Days: A Spirited Companion and Lively Muse for the Writing Life*. Novato, CA: New World Library, 1999.

Rhodes, Richard. *How to Write: Advice and Reflections*. New York: Morrow, 1995.

Roach, Mary. *Stiff: The Curious Lives of Human Cadavers*. New York: Norton, 2003.

Robinson, Roxana. *Georgia O'Keeffe: A Life*. New York: Harper & Row, 1989.

Rogak, Lisa Angowski, ed. *The Cat on My Shoulder: Writers and Their Cats*. New York: Avon Books, 1994.

Romm, Robin. *The Mercy Papers: A Memoir of Three Weeks*. New York: Scribner, 2009.

Roorbach, Bill. *Writing Life Stories*. Cincinnati: Story Press, 1998.

Rosenblatt, Roger. *Unless It Moves the Human Heart: The Craft and Art of Writing*. New York: Ecco, 2011.

Salter, James, and Robert Phelps. *Memorable Days: The Selected Letters of James Salter and Robert Phelps*. Edited by John McIntyre. Berkeley, CA: Counterpoint, 2010.

Salzman, Mark. *The Man in the Empty Boat*. New York: Open Road, 2012.

Saroyan, William. *Not Dying: A Memoir*. New York: Barricade Books, 1996.

Sarton, May. *Journal of a Solitude*. New York: Norton, 1973.

Sebold, Alice. *Lucky*. New York: Little, Brown, 2002.

See, Carolyn. *Making a Literary Life: Advice for Writers and Other Dreamers*. New York: Random House, 2002.

Sendak, Maurice. *Caldecott & Co.: Notes on Books & Pictures*. New York: Noonday Press, 1990.

Shawn, Wallace, and André Gregory. *My Dinner with André: A Screenplay*. New York: Grove Press, 1981.

Shields, Carol. *Jane Austen: A Life*. New York: Penguin, 2005.

Shields, David. *Reality Hunger: A Manifesto*. New York: Vintage Books, 2011.

Smiley, Jane. *Thirteen Ways of Looking at the Novel*. New York: Knopf, 2005.

Smith, Patti. *Just Kids*. New York: Ecco, 2010.

Stafford, William. *Writing the Australian Crawl: Views on the Writer's Vocation*. Ann Arbor: University of Michigan Press, 1978.

Stanislavski, Constantin. *An Actor Prepares*. Translated by Elizabeth Reynolds Hapgood. New York: Routledge, 1989.

Steinbeck, John. *Journal of a Novel: The East of Eden Letters*. New York: Penguin Books, 1990.

Stern, Jerome. *Making Shapely Fiction*. New York: Norton, 1991.

Sternburg, Janet, ed. *The Writer on Her Work: Contemporary Women Writers Reflect on Their Art and Situation*. New York: Norton, 1980.

Storr, Anthony. *The Dynamics of Creation*. New York: Ballantine Books, 1993.

Strickland, Bill, ed. *On Being a Writer*. Cincinnati: Writer's Digest Books, 1989.

Strunk, William, Jr., and E. B. White. *The Elements of Style*. New York: Macmillan, 1959.

Styron, William. *Havanas in Camelot: Personal Essays*. New York: Random House, 2008.

Szymborska, Wislawa. *Monologue of a Dog: New Poems*. Translated by Clare Cavanagh and Stanislaw Baranczak. Orlando, FL: Harcourt, 2006.

Tharp, Twyla. *The Creative Habit: Learn It and Use It for Life; A Practical Guide.* New York: Simon & Schuster, 2003.

Theroux, Phyllis. *The Journal Keeper: A Memoir.* New York: Atlantic Monthly Press, 2010.

Thomas, Abigail. *Thinking about Memoir.* New York: Sterling, 2008.

————. *A Three Dog Life.* Orlando, FL: Harcourt, 2006.

Tuck, Lily. "The Seducer." In *Mentors, Muses & Monsters: 30 Writers on the People Who Changed Their Lives,* edited by Elizabeth Benedict. New York: Free Press, 2009.

Ueland, Brenda. *If You Want to Write: A Book about Art, Independence and Spirit.* 2nd ed. Saint Paul, MN: Graywolf Press, 1987.

Ullmann, Liv. *Changing.* New York: Knopf, 1976.

Vann, David. *Caribou Island: A Novel.* New York: Harper, 2011.

Vida, Vendela, ed. *The Believer Book of Writers Talking to Writers.* San Francisco: Believer Books, 2007.

Villa Gillet/Le Monde, ed. *The Novelist's Lexicon: Writers on the Words That Define Their Work.* New York: Columbia University Press, 2011.

Wachtel, Eleanor. *Writers & Company.* San Diego: Harcourt Brace, 1994.

Welty, Eudora. *One Writer's Beginnings.* New York: Warner Books, 1991.

West, Jessamyn. *Hide and Seek: A Continuing Journey.* New York: Harcourt Brace Jovanovich, 1973.

Williams, Terry Tempest. "Why I Write." In *Writing Creative Nonfiction: Instruction and Insights from Teachers of the Associated Writing Programs,* edited by Carolyn Forché and Philip Gerard. Cincinnati: Story Press, 2001.

Winokur, Jon, ed. *Writers on Writing.* 3rd ed. Philadelphia: Running Press, 1990.

Wolff, Tobias. *This Boy's Life: A Memoir.* New York: Grove Press, 1989.

Woolf, Virginia. *A Writer's Diary, Being Extracts from the Diary of Virginia Woolf.* Edited by Leonard Woolf. New York: Harcourt Brace Jovanovich, 1973.

Zackheim, Victoria, ed. *He Said What? Women Write about Moments When Everything Changed.* Berkeley, CA: Seal Press, 2011.

Zinsser, William. *On Writing Well: An Informal Guide to Writing Nonfiction.* New York: Harper & Row, 1976.

————, ed. *Worlds of Childhood: The Art and Craft of Writing for Children.* Boston: Houghton Mifflin, 1990.

————. *Writing about Your Life: A Journey into the Past.* New York: Marlowe, 2004.

Index of Writers and Artists

A

Abani, Chris, 198
Ackerman, Diane, 318
Adichie, Chimamanda Ngozi, 142
Albee, Edward, 239
Alexie, Sherman, 30
Ali, Tariq, 285
Allen, Marc, 315
Allen, Woody, 310, 322
Allende, Isabel, 4, 161
Allison, Dorothy, 39, 78, 215, 306, 323
Almquist, Norma, 136
Alvarez, Julia, 94, 118, 275, 296
Andreas, Brian, 166
Angelou, Maya, 23, 156, 219, 251, 332
Aristotle, 27, 212
Armantrout, Rae, 319
Athill, Diana, 165, 338

Atkinson, Kate, 306
Atwood, Margaret, 34
Austen, Jane, 333, 335, 350
Auster, Paul, 152

B

Baker, Nicholson, 15, 23, 122, 223
Baldwin, Christina, 50
Baldwin, James, 290, 303, 333
Banville, John, 53, 195
Barker, Clive, 196
Barks, Coleman, 141
Barnes, Julian, 61, 307
Barth, John, 161
Bass, Rick, 28
Baszile, Jennifer, 21
Baudelaire, Charles, 56
Bayles, David, 92, 235, 242, 312
Beckett, Samuel, 25, 82, 126

About the Author

Barbara Abercrombie has published novels, children's picture books — including the award-winning *Charlie Anderson* — and works of nonfiction. Her personal essays have appeared in national publications as well as in many anthologies. She received the Outstanding Instructor Award and the Distinguished Instructor Award at UCLA Extension, where she teaches creative writing in the Writers' Program. She also conducts private writing retreats and writes a weekly blog at www.WritingTime.typepad.com. She lives with her husband, Robert V. Adams, and their rescue dog, Nelson, in Santa Monica, California.